Penguin Education
Penguin English Project Stage Two

Good Time
Edited by Margaret Hewitt

Chairman : Harold Rosen

Danger !
Edited by Norman Beer

Good Time
Edited by Margaret Hewitt

Openings
Edited by Alex McLeod

The Receiving End
Edited by Peter Medway

That Once Was Me
Edited by Dennis Pepper

Alone
Edited by George Robertson

Penguin English Project

Edited by Margaret Hewitt

Stage Two **Good Time**

Penguin Education

Penguin Education
A Division of Penguin Books Ltd,
Harmondsworth, Middlesex, England
Penguin Books Australia Ltd,
Ringwood, Victoria, Australia
Penguin Books Canada Ltd,
41 Steelcase Road West,
Markham, Ontario, Canada
Penguin Books (N.Z.) Ltd,
182–190 Wairau Road, Auckland, New Zealand

First published 1974
This selection copyright © Margaret Hewitt, 1974

Designed by Ivan Atanasoff
Set in Monophoto Apollo
Made and printed in Great Britain by
Butler & Tanner Ltd, Frome and London

Contents

EDWARD LUEDERS Your Poem, Man . . . *9*

BARRY HINES Excuses *10*

ALLEN EYLES Life with the Marx Brothers *12*

ADRIAN MITCHELL Leaflets *14*

JOHN TAGLIABUE On a Crowded Train One Hot Day *16*

KENNETH PATCHEN An Easy Decision *17*

R. FREEMAN Graffiti *18*

DAN LENO Dan Leno *19*

RICHARD BRAUTIGAN The Ghost Children of Tacoma *22*

ROGER MCGOUGH At Lunchtime. A Story of Love *24*

AKAHITO Haiku *25*

SAUL BELLOW Adventure of Augie March *27*

ADRIAN HENRI Tonight at Noon *30*

ANDREJ BRVAR Eeny-Meeny-Miny-Mo *31*

KALUNGANO Dream of the Black Mother *32*

AIME CESAIRE I Want to Rediscover the Secret *33*

THOMAS BERGER A Good Day to Die *35*

T. E. LAWRENCE Moving Swiftly *38*

TAMAS ST JOBY Poem Title: Two *39*

CLAUDE BROWN Saturday Night *41*

RICHARD BRAUTIGAN A Short History of Oregon *43*

ANDREW MILLS Night Fishing *46*

PABLO NERUDA Ode to the Tomato *48*

LAWRENCE FERLINGHETTI Dog *50*

JOHN TAGLIABUE Man in the Dark *52*

JOHN TAGLIABUE My Long Woollen Underwear *52*

PETE BROWN Reckless *52*

AKAHITO When I Went Out *52*

VERN RUTSALA Sunday *53*

GREGORY CORSO Secondnight in New York City after 3 Years *54*

PETE BROWN Few *54*

TOM PICKARD The Street Cleaner with his Eighteenth-Century Muck Cart *54*

ALEXANDER SOLZHENITSYN Camp Life *56*

HO CHI MINH Morning Sunshine From a Prison Diary *60*

TOM PICKARD The Daylight Hours (Song for Dole Wallas) *62*

ANONYMOUS On the Dole *63*

ANONYMOUS Driving the Bus *66*

RICHARD HILLARY Flying a Spitfire *69*

GERALD DURRELL The Collector *72*

FLANN O'BRIEN The Blondin of Dublin *77*

A.S. MAKARENKO School Play *83*

YANNIS RITSOS Carnival *86*

JEAN-PAUL SARTRE Going to a Silent Movie *88*

ANONYMOUS Going to the Pictures *90*

JEREMY SANDFORD Holiday Camps *92*

H.G. WELLS Wedding *95*

JEREMY SEABROOK Funeral *97*

PABLO NERUDA The Great Tablecloth *98*

JOHN BURNETT The Perfect Meal *99*

CHARLES MCMILLAN My Perfect Meal *101*

JEFF SAULT My Perfect Meal *101*

DAMON RUNYON A Piece of Pie *102*

TOM WOLFE Demolition Derby *108*

SUSAN VARNEY Saturday Afternoon *111*

BARRY HINES Football Match *112*

MICHAEL PARKINSON Why You Can't Have a Closet Winger in Sevenoaks *114*

ROBIN PAGE The Tin House *117*

PAUL RITCHENS Let it Flow Joe *118*

ADRIAN MITCHELL For David Mercer *119*

PABLO NERUDA Lazybones *121*

WILLIAM CARLOS WILLIAMS Heel and Toe to the End *122*

Acknowledgements *125*

List of Illustrations *127*

Index of Authors, Editors and Translators *128*

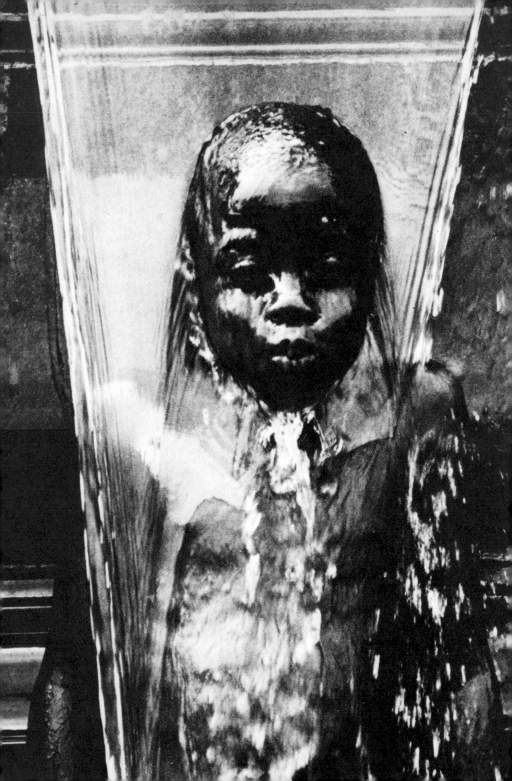

Your Poem, Man . . .

unless there's one thing seen
suddenly against another – a parsnip
sprouting for a President, or
hailstones melting in an ashtray –
nothing really happens. It takes
surprise and wild connections,
doesn't it? A walrus chewing
on a ballpoint pen. Two blue tail-
lights on Tyrannosaurus Rex. Green
cheese teeth. Maybe what we wanted
least. Or most. Some unexpected
pleats. Words that never knew
each other till right now. Plug us
into the wrong socket and see
what blows – or what lights up.
Try
    untried
        circuitry,
           new
              fuses.
Tell it like it never really was,
               man,
and maybe we can see it
          like it is.

Edward Lueders

Excuses

He missed the first lesson and Mr Rowley didn't see him until the afternoon registration.

'Were you absent this morning, Hawk?'

'I was late.'

'Does that entitle you to miss the whole first period?'

'I didn't get here till after ten.'

'I see. Just popped in for morning coffee, did you?'

'No, I was working so late last night that I laid too long. I knew we'd got history first and I was going to come without having any breakfast, but my mam wouldn't let me. I said, I've not time for

breakfast, we've got Mr Rowley first. Never mind Mr Rowley, she said, you can't go out on a morning like this wi' nowt inside you, you'll be getting run down, especially wi' all that work you're doing. Sit down and I'll make you some toast. I've no time, I said, and I was just rushing out when my dad came in from his allotment. He was nearly in tears, a dog had got into the greenhouse during the night. Come and have a look Len, he says. He's off work, you know, my dad, they're closing the pit down. Well, I could see he was upset, so I thought I'd better go and have a look. Be quick then, I said, I'm late already. It was a right mess. There were plant pots and seed boxes all over, and there must have been a dozen broken panes.

My dad was going mad. You see, with him being off work he has to do odd jobs to pass his time on, and he was going to start painting inside the greenhouse today. Well, he couldn't do a thing, state it was in and with this bad back he's got he can't do much lifting, so I thought I'd better clean up for him. Well, I couldn't very well just leave him standing there, could I? When I'd finished I had to run back home for some paper to stuff in the broken panes, and then I measured up, and went round to the plumbers to order some new glass. You've got to get your glass back in sharp, because if a wind gets up and gets inside, it'll have the lot away in no time. I was like a collier when I'd finished, so my mam made me get stripped off and have a good wash before she'd let me out into the street.'

'I see.'

'If I'd have got hold of that dog I'd have murdered it.'

'Your father will have to make sure that the door is secure in future, won't he?'

'I know, but you wouldn't think dogs'd be roaming around on such nights, would you?'

'Dogs roam around at all times, Hawk.'

'They must do, but you wouldn't think so, would you?'

'Right, you may go.'

Mr Rowley stayed to complete the register, and the class dismissed.

Barry Hines *The Blinder*

Life with the Marx Brothers

Groucho is explaining to Chico his plan for developing the Coconut district and he has a map spread out on a table.

GROUCHO Now here is a little peninsula, and here is a viaduct leading over to the mainland.

CHICO Why a duck?

GROUCHO I'm all right. How are you? I say here is a little peninsula and here is a viaduct leading over to the mainland.

CHICO All right, why a duck?

GROUCHO I'm not playing ask me another. I say that's a viaduct.

CHICO All right. Why a duck? Why a duck, why-a no chicken?

GROUCHO Well, I don't know why-a no chicken. I'm a stranger here myself. All I know is that it's a viaduct. You try to cross over there a chicken and you'll find out vy-a-duck.

CHICO When I go some place I just –

GROUCHO It's deep water, that's vy-a-duck. Deep water. Look, look suppose you were out horseback riding and you came to that stream and you wanted to ford over. You couldn't make it. It's too deep.

CHICO What-a you want with a Ford if you gotta horse?

GROUCHO Well, I'm sorry the matter ever came up. All I know is that it's a viaduct.

CHICO I know. All right, I catch on why a horse, why a chicken, why this, why that. I no catch on why a duck.

GROUCHO I was only fooling. I was only fooling. They're going to build a tunnel there in the morning. Now is that clear to you?

CHICO Yes, everything except why a duck.

GROUCHO Well, that's fine. Then we can go ahead with this thing.

After some badinage, quite lost on Chico, about giving him a preferential burial in the local cemetery, Groucho returns to the point and gives Chico directions on how to reach the auction ground.

GROUCHO Now you know how to get down there. Now look, now look here, you go down that narrow path there until you come to that little jungle there – you see it? Where those thatched palms are. Then there's a little clearing there, a little clearing with a wire fence around it. You see that wire fence there?

CHICO All right, why a fence?

GROUCHO Oh no, we're not going to go through all that again.

Allen Eyles *The Marx Brothers: Their World of Comedy*

Leaflets

Outside the plasma supermarket
I stretch out my arm to the shoppers and say:
'Can I give you one of these?'
I give each of them a leaf from a tree.

The first shopper thanks me.

The second puts the leaf in his mack pocket where his wife won't see.

The third says she is not interested in leaves. She looks like a mutilated willow.

The fourth says: 'Is it art?' I say that it is a leaf.

The fifth looks through his leaf and smiles at the light beyond.

The sixth hurls down his leaf and stamps it till dark purple mud oozes through.

The seventh says she will press it in her album.

The eighth complains that it is an oak leaf and says she would be on my side if I were also handing out birch leaves, apple leaves, privet leaves, and larch leaves. I say that it is a leaf.

The ninth takes the leaf carefully and then, with a backhand fling, gives it its freedom.

It glides, following surprise curving alleys through the air. It lands. I pick it up.

The tenth reads both sides of the leaf twice and then says: 'Yes, but it doesn't say who we should kill.'

But you took your leaf like a kiss.

They tell me that on Saturdays,
You can be seen in your own city centre
Giving away forests, orchards, jungles.

Adrian Mitchell

On a Crowded Train One Hot Day

An
old
man
from
the
sea
with
a
green
face
enters
the
subway
train
with
a
paper
bag
smelling
of
fish
and
before
you
know
it
every
body
emerges
from
the
train
with
a
wet
fish.

John Tagliabue

An Easy Decision

I had finished my dinner
Gone for a walk
It was fine
Out and I started whistling

It wasn't long before

I met a
Man and his wife riding on
A pony with seven
Kids running along beside them

I said hello and
Went on
Pretty soon I met another
Couple
This time with nineteen
Kids and all of them
Riding on
A big smiling hippopotamus
I invited them home

Kenneth Patchen

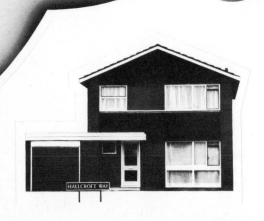

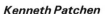

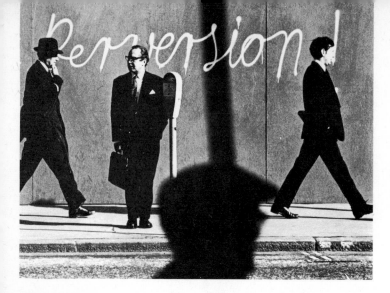

Graffiti

'In fifteen years on the beat,' said the burly PC, tucking in his chin, 'I've never yet caught anyone at it.' Only two feet away from him WHY VOTE–? MAKE IT A DOUBLE X had been stencilled on the wall. . . .

The manager of a busy Knightsbridge pub answered 'It's uncanny. As though they were written by an invisible man. I'm always popping down to the cellar here, and always glance into the gents as I go past, and I've never seen anyone writing on the wall. Ten years I've been here.'

A seventeen-year-old student says his drawings are 'done under pressure' – hoping a police officer won't come round the corner. The artist usually works at about 10 p.m., 'on my way home', and never knows until he starts what he intends to do; 'I have a mechanical reaction to improve – or deface – I don't want to sound vain.' Obscene additions by others add to his difficulties.

'I love these ads,' he says. 'They leave plenty of space for me to draw on. My only complaint is they are not changed often enough. I should really be in advertising, I suppose. I would design posters with huge loopholes for other people to fill up.'

In 1960 Finch's installed a blackboard, and provided the chalk to write on it, in the gents of the Black Horse, in Marylebone. They hoped to divert a lot of writing from the lavatory walls on to something that was easier to clean. All that happened, in fact, was that a lot of chalk was pinched.

R. Freeman

Dan Leno

I was about seventeen when I was seized with a restless desire to roll on the ocean waves. I was in Liverpool at the time, and a friend persuaded me to set out with him for the pearl fisheries situated between Margate and Japan.

When we had got about as far as New Brighton after a fair passage, with the wind north-north by south-south, latitude nineteen and six, longitude three foot four, sea calm but dirty owing to it being the bathing season, a tempest arose. The ship gave a violent heave, as if it wasn't comfortable in its seat, and I pitched head first into my friend, and we both went rolling on the floor, under a shower of tin-cans and bottles from the shelves.

My friend got up and tried to look as though he had been doing this all his life. He opened a bottle of ale, and asked me what would I have. I thanked him kindly and said I would like a bucket, which he got me, and lashed me to it in case I should fall overboard and miss it.

Now I come to the most exciting part of the voyage. The captain was a reckless dare-devil sort of navvy, and he had decided to take a short cut across the Bospherranean, knowing all the time the fearful risk he was running of going too close to the Magnetic Islands. The drawing powers of these islands are so strong that they have the 'House Full' boards out every day. No steel or iron can pass within three streets of them. We could see far-off through our opera glasses that there were half a dozen ironclads sticking to the rocks, deserted by their crews. But our careless captain only laughed and said his ship was all wood, and we were quite safe.

But we had only got half-way past the islands, when suddenly we were very much surprised to see our paddle-wheels suddenly fly off the ship and go straight to land. We were simply thunderstruck. Then the funnel flew out and stuck to some trees, then away went the anchor. Next, the buttons off the sailors' clothes shot off, and fell like a shower of hail on the rocks, and there they stuck, glittering in the sunlight. It was a pretty sight but still buttons are buttons – I won't labour the point.

Then there was poor old Ben Bowsprit, the bosun. He was wearing a pair of hob-nailed boots at the time, and the magnetism dragged him off the ship, feet foremost. When he reached the island, he stuck to the same rocks by his feet, and was hanging head downwards until he could unlace his boots, drop into the sea, and swim back to the ship. The ultimate disaster was all owing to Ben's fatal passion for wearing these hob-nailed boots. For when he reached the ship again, it happened that all the nails had naturally been drawn out of the vessel by the islands, and when Ben took hold of the ship to pull himself on board it came to pieces in his hand, and we all found ourselves struggling in the ocean. I always blamed Ben for that.

Every one of us was drowned except myself, and I was saved by floating to the islands on a drawing-room door. Of course I did my best for the crew. I pulled out my note book and took down their last farewells in a sort of shorthand, and there wasn't one that I didn't say a kind word to. But I had in my hand a rolling pin out of the kitchen and when any of the poor fellows caught hold of my raft, I had the presence of mind to hit them till they let go. You see, I had to be saved, because I was engaged to appear at a Liverpool hall, and I try never to disappoint the public.

Dan Leno Hys Book

John Glashan

The Ghost Children of Tacoma

The children of Tacoma, Washington, went to war in December 1941. It seemed like the thing to do, following in the footsteps of their parents and other grown-ups who acted as if they knew what was happening.

'Remember Pearl Harbor!' they said.

'You bet!' we said.

I was a child, then, though now I look like somebody else. We were at war in Tacoma. Children can kill imaginary enemies just as well as adults can kill real enemies. It went on for years.

During the Second World War, I personally killed 352,892 enemy soldiers without wounding one. Children need a lot less hospitals in war than grown-ups do. Children pretty much look at it from the all-death side.

I sank 987 battleships, 532 aircraft carriers, 799 cruisers, 2007 destroyers and 161 transport ships. Transports were not too interesting a target: very little sport.

I also sank 5465 enemy PT boats. I have no idea why I sank so many of them. It was just one of those things. Every time I turned around for four years, I was sinking a PT boat. I still wonder about that. 5465 are a lot of PT boats.

I only sank three submarines. Submarines were just not up my alley. I sank my first submarine in the spring of 1942. A lot of kids rushed out and sank submarines right and left during December and January. I waited.

I waited until April, and then one morning on my way to school: BANG! my first sub, right in front of a grocery store. I sank my second submarine in 1944. I could afford to wait two years before sinking another one.

I sank my last submarine in February 1945, a few days after my tenth birthday. I was not totally satisfied with the presents I got that year.

And then there was the sky! I ventured forth into the sky, seeking the enemy there, while Mount Rainier towered up like a cold white general in the background.

I was an ace pilot with my P-38 and my Grumman Wildcat, my P-51 Mustang and my Messerschmitt. That's right: Messerschmitt. I captured one and had it painted a special color, so my own men wouldn't try to shoot me down by mistake. Everybody recognized my Messerschmitt and the enemy had hell to pay for it.

I shot down 8942 fighter planes, 6420 bombers and fifty-one blimps.
I shot down most of the blimps when the war was first in season.
Later, sometime in 1943, I stopped shooting down blimps altogether.

Too slow.

I also destroyed 1281 tanks, 777 bridges and 109 oil refineries
because I knew we were in the right.

'Remember Pearl Harbor!' they said.

'You bet!' we said.

I shot the enemy planes down by holding out my arms straight from
my body and running like hell, shouting at the top of my lungs:
R A T-tattattattattattattattattattattattat!

Children don't do that kind of stuff any more. Children do other
things now and because children do other things now, I have whole
days when I feel like the ghost of a child, examining the memory of
toys played back into the earth again.

There was a thing I used to do that was also a lot of fun when I was
a young aeroplane. I used to hunt up a couple of flashlights and hold
them lit in my hands at night, with my arms straight out from my
body and be a night pilot zooming down the streets of Tacoma.

I also used to play aeroplane in the house, too, by taking four chairs
from the kitchen and putting them together: two chairs facing the
same way for the fuselage and a chair for each wing.

In the house I played mostly at dive-bombing. The chairs seemed to
do that best. My sister used to sit in the seat right behind me and
radio urgent messages back to base.

'We only have one bomb left, but we can't let the aircraft carrier
escape. We'll have to drop the bomb down the smoke-stack. Over.
Thank you, Captain, we'll need all the luck we can get. Over and
out.'

Then my sister would say to me, 'Do you think you can do it?' and
I'd reply, 'Of course, hang onto your hat.'

Your Hat
Gone Now These
Twenty Years
1 January 1965

Richard Brautigan *Revenge of the Lawn*

At Lunchtime.
A Story of Love

When the busstopped suddenly to avoid damaging a mother and child in the road, the younglady in the greenhat sitting opposite was thrown across me, and not being one to miss an opportunity i started to makelove with all my body.

At first she resisted saying that it was tooearly in the morning and toosoon after breakfast and that anyway she found me repulsive. But when i explained that this being a nuclearage, the world was going to end at lunchtime, she tookoff her greenhat, put her busticket in her pocket and joined in the exercise.

The buspeople, and therewere many of them, were shockedandsurprised and amused-andannoyed, but when the word got around that the world was coming to an end at lunch-time, they put their pride in their pockets with their bustickets and madelove one with the other. And even the busconductor, being over, climbed into the cab and struck up some sort of relationship with the driver.

Thatnight, on the bus coming home, wewere all alittle embarrassed, especially me and the younglady in the greenhat, and we all started to say in different ways howhasty and foolish we had been. Butthen, always having been a bitofalad, i stood up and said it was a pity that the world didn't nearly end every lunchtime and that we could always pretend. And then it happened . . .

Quick asa crash we all changed partners and soon the bus was aquiver with white mothballbodies doing naughty things.

And the next day
And everyday
In everybus
In everystreet
Ineverytown
In everycountry

people pretended that the world was coming to an end at lunchtime. It still hasn't. Although in a way it has.

Roger McGough

Haiku

I wish I were close
To you as the wet skirt of
A salt girl to her body.
I think of you always.

Akahito *Translated from the Japanese by Kenneth Rexroth*

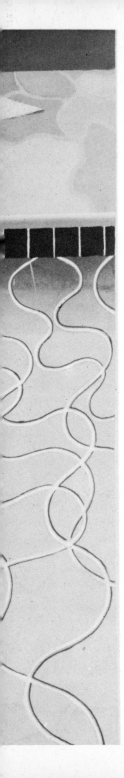

Adventure of Augie March

(Augie is on holiday at an expensive resort, having been invited to act as chauffeur to a very rich woman named Mrs Renling.)

But there were people at the table near theirs that soon were of more interest to me – two young girls, of beauty to put a stop to such thoughts or drive them to the dwindling point. There was a moment when I could have fallen for either one of them, and then everything bent to one side, towards the slenderer, slighter, younger one. I fell in love with her, and not in the way I had loved Hilda Novinson either, going like a satellite on the back of the streetcar or sticking around her father's tailor shop. This time I had a different kind of maniac energy and knew what sexual sting was. . . . So I was dragged, entrained, over a barrel. And I had a special handicap, because of the way I presented myself – due to Mrs Renling – as if God had not left out a single one of His gifts, and I was advertising His liberality with me : good looks, excellent wardrobe, mighty fine manners, social ease, wittiness, handsome-devil smiles, neat dancing and address with women – all in the freshest gold-leaf. And the trouble was that I had what you might call forged credentials. It was my worry that Esther Fenchel would find this out. . . .

And I behaved ingeniously too. I got into conversations with old Fenchel, not the girls' father but their uncle, who was in the mineral-water business. It wasn't easy, because he was a millionaire. He drove a Packard, the same model and colour as the Renlings' ; I parked behind him on the drive so that he had to look twice to see which was his, and then I had him. *Inter pares.* For how could he tell that I earned twenty-five dollars a week and didn't own the car ?

We talked. I offered him a Perfecto Queen. He smiled it away; he had his own tailor-made Havanas in a case big enough for a pistol, and he was so ponderously huge it didn't even bulge in his pocket. His face was fat and seamed, black-eyed – eyes black as the meat of Chinese litchi nuts – with grey, heinie hair, clipped to the fat of the scalp, back and sides. It was a little discouraging that the girls were his heiresses, as he right away told me, probably guessing that I wasn't bringing out the bower of my charm for his old cartilage-heavy Rembrandt of a squash nose with its white hairs and gunpowder speckles. To be sure not. And he wanted me to know in what league I was playing. I didn't give an inch. I've never backed down from male relatives, either calf or bull, or let father and guardians discomfit me.

Getting to Esther's aunt was harder, since she was sickly, timid, and silent, with the mood of rich people whose health lets them down. Her clothes and jewellery were fine, but the poor lady's face was full of private effort; she was a little deaf from it. I didn't have to put on friendly interest; I really (God knows from where) had it. And by instinct I knew that what would fetch her – as infirm, loaded with dough, and beaten a long way out of known channels by the banked spoon-oars of special silver as she was – was the charm of ordinary health. So I talked away to her and was pretty acceptable.

'My dear Augie, was that Mrs Fenchel you were sitting with?' said Mrs Renling. 'She hasn't done anything but watch the sprinkler all month, so I thought she was screwloose. Did you speak to her first?'

'Well, I just happened to be sitting by her.'

I got a good mark for this; she was pleased. But the next thing to be thought of was my purpose, and this she immediately and roughly found out. 'It's the girls, isn't it! Well, they are very beautiful, aren't they? Especially the black-haired one. Gorgeous. And mischievous, full of the devil she looks. But remember, Augie, you're with me; I'm responsible for your behaviour. And the girl is not a waitress, and you better not think you-know-what. My dear boy, you're very clever and good, and I want to see you get ahead. I'll see that you do. Naturally, with this girl, you haven't got a chance.'

But Mrs Renling wasn't infallible, and had already made one mistake, that of thinking it was Thea rather than Esther Fenchel I was in love with. Also, she had no notion how much in love I was, down to the poetic threat of death. I didn't want her to have any notion either, though I would have been happy to tell someone. I did not like what I foresaw Mrs Renling would make of it, and so I was satisfied to let her think it was Thea, the kinky-haired but also glorious-looking sister I carried the torch for, and I used some deceit. It didn't take much, as it was pleasing to Mrs Renling's pride to think she had guessed, quick and infallible, what was bothering me.

As a matter of fact Thea Fenchel was better than merely pleasant to me, and I was fishing after her uncle, who was in a bad mood, surly and difficult, one morning, when she asked me whether I played tennis. I had to say, and though it was a bad moment for me, smiling, that riding was my sport; and I desperately thought that I must get a racket and go at once to the public courts in Benton Harbour to learn. Not that I had been born to the saddle either; but it covered my origins somewhat to say that I was a horseman and had a pretty creditable clang.

'My partner hasn't come,' said Thea, 'and Esther's on the beach.'

Within ten minutes I too was on the sand, notwithstanding that I had promised to play cards with Mrs Renling after her mineral bath, when, she said, she felt too weakened to read. . . .

Presently she went up; and so did I, a littler later. Mrs Renling gave me the icy treatment for being late. And, I thought, lying on the floor of my room with my heels upon the bedspread like an armoured man fallen from his horse, spur-tangled and needing block and tackle to be raised, that it was time, seeing my inattention was making Mrs Renling angry, to have some progress to show for it at least. I got up and brushed myself without particular heart or interest, using two military brushes she had given me. I went down in the slow, white elevator and, on the ground floor, moseyed around in the lobby.

It was sundown, near dinner-time, with brilliant darkening water, napkins and broad menus standing up in the dining-room, and roses and ferns in long-necked vases, the orchestra tuning back of its curtain. I was alone in the corridor, troubled and rocky, and trod on slowly to the music room, where the phonograph was playing Caruso. . . . Resting her elbows on the closed cabinet, in a white suit and round white hat, next thing to a bishop's biretta, bead-embroidered, was Esther Fenchel; she stood with one foot set on its point.

I said, 'Miss Fenchel, I wonder if you would like to go with me some evening to the House of David.' Astonished, she looked up from the music. 'They have dancing every night.'

I saw nothing but failure, from the first word out, and felt smitten, pounded from all sides.
'With you? I should say not. I certainly won't.'

Saul Bellow *Adventures of Augie March*

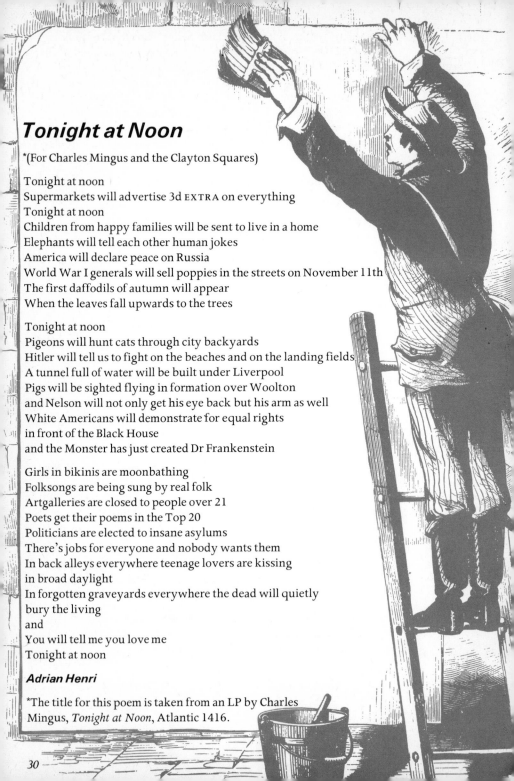

Tonight at Noon

*(For Charles Mingus and the Clayton Squares)

Tonight at noon
Supermarkets will advertise 3d EXTRA on everything
Tonight at noon
Children from happy families will be sent to live in a home
Elephants will tell each other human jokes
America will declare peace on Russia
World War I generals will sell poppies in the streets on November 11th
The first daffodils of autumn will appear
When the leaves fall upwards to the trees

Tonight at noon
Pigeons will hunt cats through city backyards
Hitler will tell us to fight on the beaches and on the landing fields
A tunnel full of water will be built under Liverpool
Pigs will be sighted flying in formation over Woolton
and Nelson will not only get his eye back but his arm as well
White Americans will demonstrate for equal rights
in front of the Black House
and the Monster has just created Dr Frankenstein

Girls in bikinis are moonbathing
Folksongs are being sung by real folk
Artgalleries are closed to people over 21
Poets get their poems in the Top 20
Politicians are elected to insane asylums
There's jobs for everyone and nobody wants them
In back alleys everywhere teenage lovers are kissing
in broad daylight
In forgotten graveyards everywhere the dead will quietly
bury the living
and
You will tell me you love me
Tonight at noon

Adrian Henri

*The title for this poem is taken from an LP by Charles
Mingus, *Tonight at Noon*, Atlantic 1416.

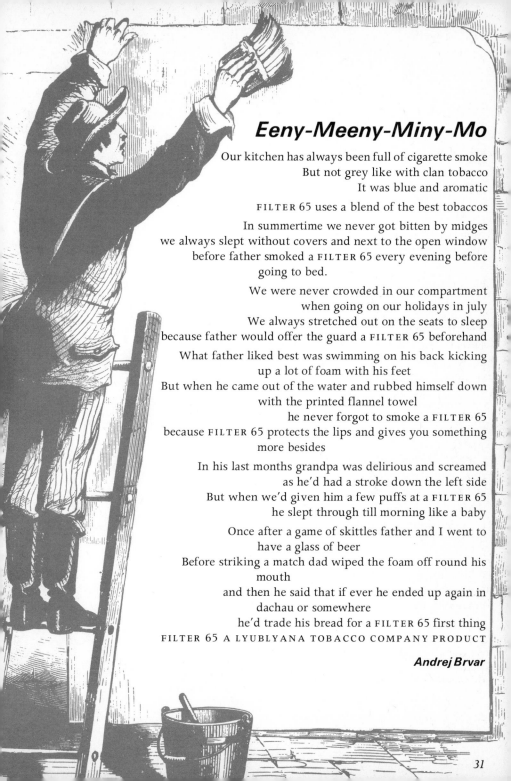

Eeny-Meeny-Miny-Mo

Our kitchen has always been full of cigarette smoke
But not grey like with clan tobacco
It was blue and aromatic

FILTER 65 uses a blend of the best tobaccos

In summertime we never got bitten by midges
we always slept without covers and next to the open window
before father smoked a FILTER 65 every evening before
going to bed.

We were never crowded in our compartment
when going on our holidays in july
We always stretched out on the seats to sleep
because father would offer the guard a FILTER 65 beforehand

What father liked best was swimming on his back kicking
up a lot of foam with his feet
But when he came out of the water and rubbed himself down
with the printed flannel towel
he never forgot to smoke a FILTER 65
because FILTER 65 protects the lips and gives you something
more besides

In his last months grandpa was delirious and screamed
as he'd had a stroke down the left side
But when we'd given him a few puffs at a FILTER 65
he slept through till morning like a baby

Once after a game of skittles father and I went to
have a glass of beer
Before striking a match dad wiped the foam off round his
mouth
and then he said that if ever he ended up again in
dachau or somewhere
he'd trade his bread for a FILTER 65 first thing
FILTER 65 A LYUBLYANA TOBACCO COMPANY PRODUCT

Andrej Brvar

31

Dream of the Black Mother

To my Mother

Black mother
Rocks her son
And in her black head
Covered with black hair
She keeps marvellous dreams.

Black mother
Rocks her son
And forgets
That the earth has dried up the maize
That yesterday the groundnuts were finished.

She dreams of marvellous worlds
Where her son would go to school
To school where men study.

Black mother
Rocks her son
And forgets
Her brothers building towns and cities
Cementing them with their blood.

She dreams of marvellous worlds
Where her son would run along the street
The street where men pass by.

Black mother
Rocks her son
And listening
To the voice from afar
Brought by the wind.

She dreams of marvellous worlds,
Marvellous worlds
Where her son will be able to live.

Kalungano *Translated from the French by Philippa Rumsey*

I Want to Rediscover the Secret

I want to rediscover the secret of great speech and of great burning.
I want to say storm. I want to say river. I want to say tornado. I want
to say leaf, I want to say tree. I want to be soaked by every rainfall,
moistened by every dew. As frenetic blood rolls on the slow current
of the eye, I want to roll words like maddened horses like new
children like clotted milk like curfew like traces of a temple like
precious stones buried deep enough to daunt all miners. The man
who couldn't understand me couldn't understand the roaring of a
tiger.

Aimé Césaire *Return to My Native Land*
Translated from the French by John Berger and Anna Bostock

A Good Day to Die

'Grandfather,' I said, 'I think it is a good day to die.'

You tell that to an Indian, and he don't immediately begin soothing you or telling you you're wrong, that everything's going to be swell, etc., for it ain't the hollow speech it would be among whites. Nor is it suicidal, like somebody who takes the attitude that life has gone stale for him, so he's going to throw it over. What it means is you will fight until you're all used up. Far from being sour, life is so sweet you will live it to the hilt and be consumed by it. One time before I joined the tribe a band of Cheyenne caught the cholera from some emigrants and those that wasn't yet dying got into battle dress, mounted their war ponies, and challenged the invisible disease to come out and fight like a man.

The troops reached the river about two miles to the west and then began to move downstream towards us. They knowed we was in the vicinity but it held a certain surprise for them to come round a bend of the Solomon and find three hundred Cheyenne horsemen waiting in line of battle, our left flank against the river and our right under the bluffs.

The Human Beings was in full regalia, warriors and ponies painted, feathers galore, a good many in the full bonnet, the sun picking up the gaudy colors and glinting off lance heads and musket barrels. Some of the braves was talking to their horses, those animals prancing and breathing through expanded nostrils as if they was already charging. They smelled the big cavalry mounts and began fiercely to whinny, having the same attitude to them that the human Cheyenne had to the whites.

I was riding a buckskin, one of those taken in that Crow raid, and he was a mighty good animal though having to make his way through life without much commentary aside from the normal greetings. Right now was the closest I ever come to discussing philosophical matters with him. I was real nervous – owing to my suspicion that not all my comrades took Old Lodge Skin's position on my presence in the middle of the first rank. Especially Younger Bear, who had been down on the right wing but seeing me rode up and wedged a place for his pony alongside. He was painted dead black from waist up, with vermilion in the part of his hair, his eyes outlined in white and horizontal white bars across his cheeks.

I couldn't tell whether he was grinning at me or just baring his teeth; it was the first notice he had paid me in a long time. I didn't return it; I wasn't feeling at all well, and was sure grateful for the war paint I had on myself. That's the wonderful thing about paint; no matter how you feel inside, you will still look horrible.

Hump and the other fighting leaders was riding up and down the line and the medicine man Ice was also there, uttering his mumbo-jumbo and shaking rattles, buffalo tails and other junk towards the cavalry, which had stopped a half mile away on the bottom and seemed to be just studying us. I was hoping they would maybe start laughing themselves to death: the soldiers, I mean. Because that's what I was inclined to do. You get this funny excitement before a charge; and the longer it takes to get under way, the more intense it becomes, so that when you finally go, you are doing what you need more than anything in the world at that point.

But add to the situation that I was naked and wearing the plug hat, that we was facing some three or four hundred white men carrying firearms, and that I was in my fifth year of pretending to be an Indian – I found myself laughing my guts out no doubt preparatory to their being filled with hot lead.

However, I did my best to muffle this, so that it sounded like a mumble or a deep guttural chant as a matter of fact, like a natural Cheyenne thing. It seemed to impress Younger Bear, for he took it up, and then the next braves on either side, and pretty soon it was sounding from every chest and had turned into the Cheyenne war song, and we began to move forward on its music at the walk, some of the ponies dancing out but the front rank generally dressed. We was still holding back our power, bottling it up while working the charm, paralysing them whites by our magic as we walked in the sacred way.

I forgot about myself, being just a part of the mystical circle in which the Cheyenne believed they were continuously joined which is the round of the earth and the sun, and life and death too, for the disjunction between them is a matter of appearance and not the true substance, so that every Cheyenne who has ever lived and those now living make one people: the invulnerable, invincible Human Beings, of all nature the supreme product.

We had proceeded maybe two–three hundred yards in this fashion, the troops still watching us, obviously charmed like the antelope in that surround and about to be similarly butchered – a number of our warriors had indeed slung their bows and were grasping war clubs and hatchets, expecting to knock the helpless soldiers from the saddle – when there was a multiple glitter from the blue ranks and above our song come the brass staccato of the bugle call.

They had drawn sabres and next they charged.

We stopped. There was six hundred yards of river bottom between them and us. Soon it was down to four, then three, and our singing petered out. The bugle was done by now, and no sound was heard but the thumping of a thousand iron-shod hoofs intermixed with scabbard jangle. And speaking for myself I never saw guidons nor uniforms nor even horses but rather a sort of device, one big mowing machine with many hundred bright blades that chopped into dust all life before it and spewed it out behind for a quarter mile of rising yellow cloud.

Now we was the paralysed, and froze to our ground until the oncoming ranks was within one hundred yards, then seventy-five, and then we burst into fragments and fled in uttermost rout. The magic, you see, had been good against bullets, not the long knives.

Thomas Berger *Little Big Man*

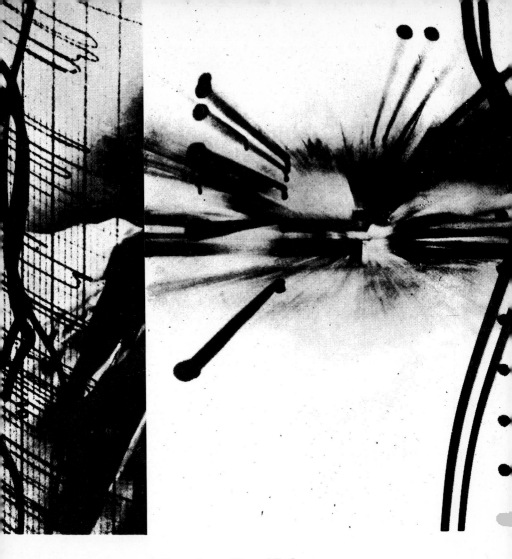

Moving Swiftly

It's usually my satisfaction to purr along gently about 60 m.p.h. drinking in the air and the general view. I lose detail even at such moderate speeds but gain comprehension. When I open out a little more, as for instance across Salisbury Plain at 80 or so, I feel the earth moulding herself under me. It is me piling up this hill, hollowing this valley, stretching out this level place. Almost the earth comes alive, heaving and tossing on each side like a sea. That's a thing that the slowcoach will never feel. It is the reward of speed. I could write you pages on the lustfulness of moving swiftly.

T.E. Lawrence

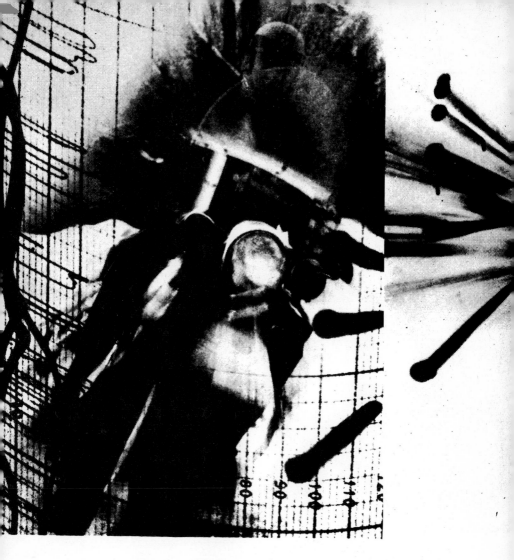

Poem Title: Two

You will experience this poem if
    You take an approximately 1·5 × 0·7 meter nylon bag,
    Fill it up with fine sand,
    Tie its mouth,
    Lay it on a table in your bathroom and
    With a single stroke of a Nineteenth-Century Austrian cavalry
      sabre,
    Cut it in two.

Tamas St Joby

Saturday Night

Saturday night. I suppose there's a Saturday night in every Negro community throughout the nation just like Saturday night in Harlem. The bars will jump. The precinct station will have a busy night. The hospital's emergency ward will jump.

Cats who have been working all their lives, who've never been in any trouble before, good-doing righteous cats, self-respecting, law-abiding citizens – they'll all come out. Perhaps it'll be their night in the bar, their night in the police station, maybe their night in the emergency ward. . . .

To me, it always seemed as though Saturday night was the down-home night. In the tales I'd heard about down-home – how so-and-so got bad and killed Cousin Joe or knocked out Cousin Willie's eye – everything violent happened on Saturday night. It was the only time for anything to really happen, because people were too tired working all week from sunup to sundown to raise but so much hell on the week nights. Then, comes Saturday, and they take it kind of easy during the day, resting up for another Saturday night.

Down home, when they went to town, all the niggers would just break bad, so it seemed. Everybody just seemed to let out all their hostility on everybody else. Maybe they were hoping that they could get their throat cut. Perhaps if a person was lucky enough to get his throat cut, he'd be free from the fields. On the other hand, if someone was lucky enough to cut somebody else's throat, he'd done the guy a favor, because he'd freed him. . . .

Saturday night is a time to try new things. Maybe that's why so many people in the older generation had to lose their lives on

Saturday night. It must be something about a Saturday night with Negroes . . . Maybe they wanted to die on Saturday night. They'd always associated Sunday with going to heaven, because that was when they went to church and sang all those songs, clapped and shouted and stomped their feet and praised the Lord. Maybe they figured that if they died on Sunday morning, the Lord's day, they'd be well on their way.

Everybody has this thing about Saturday night. I imagine that before pot or horse or any other drugs hit Harlem good and strong, the people just had to try something else, like knifing or shooting somebody, because Saturday night was the night for daring deeds. Since there was no pot out on a large scale then, I suppose one of the most daring deeds anyone could perform was to shoot or stab somebody. . . .

People know you shouldn't bother with Negroes on Saturday night, because for some reason or another, Negroes just don't mind dying on Saturday night. They seem ready to die, so they're not going to take but so much stuff. There were some people who were always trying to get themselves killed. Every Saturday night, they'd try it all over again.

One was Big Bill. When I was just a kid on Eighth Avenue in knee pants, this guy was trying to get himself killed. He was always in some fight with a knife. He was always cutting or trying to cut somebody's throat. He was always getting cut or getting stabbed, getting hit in the head, getting shot. Every Saturday night that he was out there, something happened. If you heard on Sunday morning that somebody had gotten shot or stabbed, you didn't usually ask who did it. You'd ask if Big Bill did it. If he did it, no one paid too much attention to it, because he was always doing something like that. They'd say, 'Yeah, man. That cat is crazy.'

If somebody else had done it, you'd wonder why, and this was something to talk about and discuss. Somebody else might not have been as crazy. In the case of Big Bill, everybody expected that sooner or later somebody would kill him and put him out of his misery and that this was what he was trying for. One time Spanish Joe stabbed him. He just missed his lung, and everybody thought he was going to cool it behind that. But as soon as the cat got back on the street, he was right out there doing it again.

Even now, he's always getting in fights out on the streets on Saturday nights. He's always hurting somebody, or somebody's hurting him. He just seems to be hanging on. I think he's just unlucky. Here's a cat who's been trying to get himself killed every Saturday night as far back as I can remember, and he still hasn't made it. I suppose you've got to sympathize with a guy like that, because he's really been trying.

Claude Brown *Manchild in the Promised Land*

A Short History of Oregon

I would do things like that when I was sixteen. I'd hitch-hike fifty miles in the rain to go hunting for the last hours of the day. I'd stand alongside the road with a 30:30 and my thumb out and think nothing of it, expecting to be picked up and I always was.

'Where are you going?'

'Deer hunting.'

That meant something in Oregon.

'Get in.'

It was raining like hell when I got out of the car at the top of the ridge. The driver couldn't believe it. I saw a draw half-full of trees, sloping down into a valley obscured by rain mist.

I hadn't the slightest idea where the valley led to. I'd never been there before and I didn't care.

'Where are you going?' the driver said, hardly believing that I was getting out of the car in the rain.

'Down there.'

When he drove off I was alone in the mountains and that was how I wanted it to be. I was waterproofed from head to toe and had some candy bars in my pocket.

I walked down through the trees, trying to kick a deer out of the dry thickets, but it didn't really make any difference if I saw one or not.

I just wanted the awareness of hunting. The thought of the deer being there was just as good as the deer actually being there.

There was nothing stirring in the thickets. I didn't see any sign of a deer or the sign of a bird or the sign of a rabbit or anything.

Sometimes I would just stand there. The trees were dripping. There was only the sign of myself: alone, so I ate a candy bar.

I had no idea of the time. The sky was dark with winter rain. I only had a couple of hours when I started and I could feel that they were nearly at an end and soon it would be night.

I came out of a thicket into a patch of stumps and a logging road that curved down into the valley. They were new stumps. The trees had been cut sometime that year. Perhaps in the spring. The road curved into the valley.

The rain slackened off, then stopped and a strange kind of silence settled over everything. It was twilight and wouldn't last long. There was a turn in the logging road and suddenly, without warning, there was a house right there in the middle of my private nowhere. I didn't like it.

The house was more of a large shack than anything else with a lot of old cars surrounding it and there was all sorts of logging junk and things that you need and then abandon after using.

I didn't want the house to be there. The rain mist lifted and I looked back up the mountain. I'd come down only about half a mile, thinking all the time I was alone.

That was a joke.

There was a window in the house-shack facing up the road toward me. I couldn't see anything in the window. Even though it was starting to get night, they hadn't turned their lights on yet. I knew there was somebody home because heavy black smoke was coming out of the chimney.

As I got closer to the house, the front door slammed open and a kid ran out onto a crude makeshift porch. He didn't have any shoes or a coat on. He was about nine years old and his blond hair was dishevelled as if the wind were blowing all the time in his hair.

He looked older than nine and was immediately joined by three sisters who were three, five and seven. The sisters weren't wearing any shoes either and they didn't have any coats on. The sisters looked older than they were.

The quiet spell of the twilight broke suddenly and it started raining again, but the kids didn't go into the house. They just stood there on the porch, getting all wet and looking at me.

I'll have to admit that I was a strange sight coming down their muddy little road in the middle of God-damn nowhere with darkness coming on and a 30:30 cradled down in my arms, so the night rain wouldn't get in the barrel.

The kids didn't say a word as I walked by. The sisters' hair was unruly like dwarf witches'. I didn't see their folks. There was no light on in the house.

A Model A truck lay on its side in front of the house. It was next to three empty fifty-gallon oil drums. They didn't have a purpose any more. There were some odd pieces of rusty cable. A yellow dog came out and stared at me.

I didn't say a word in my passing. The kids were soaking wet now. They huddled together in silence on the porch. I had no reason to believe that there was anything more to life than this.

Richard Brautigan *Revenge of the Lawn*

Night Fishing

My friend George . . . and Stephen picked me up at half past six
and we set out in the car for our night's fishing. We reached Walton-
on-Thames at about eight o'clock. We jumped out of the car and
opened the boot and got our fishing gear out. We started walking
along the river looking for a dry spot to fish. As soon as we found our
spot we had to light the hurricane lamps up. After that we set up our
rods. All three of us set up ledger rods, because if we done float
fishing it would be too dark to see the float. I set up my rod which
consisted of a rod, reel, line, ledger, split shot and a hook with a
maggot on one end. I was now ready to cast out. I heard the splash
but could not see where it went, but that did not matter. All that
remained now was to fit my bite indicator, which was a bit of bread.
You pulled the line down just by the reel and squeezed the bread
round the line. The weight of the bread took the line down towards
the ground, so you must always keep your eye on the bread, because
if there is a fish round the maggot he will first smell it and then take
it in his mouth and then swim away pulling the line up, and wallop
you strike, and he is on. Strike I did. 'I've got one' I shouted. I
started reeling in feeling no tension on the line so I thought he had got
away. But I had hooked him, it was a barbel. I tried to get the hook
out but he had took it right down, so I got my disgorger out and tried
to get the hook out with that, but that did not also work. So I had to
break the line leaving the hook inside the fish. I threw him back in
the river, he was still splashing about on the surface an hour later. It
was now about twelve o'clock and I was the only one who had
caught one. About half-twelve Steve caught one. He reeled in. This
was also a barbel. The hook was just inside the mouth. So Steve
could easy free the hook. Eventually all three of us had caught one,
they were all barbel. It was now very cold and dark. Steve and
George said they would go and get some wood for a fire. They brought
back a big pile of wood. I put my rod down and built a fire. I poured
paraffin on the wood and put a match to it. It went up in flames. We
all sat round it. A mist was now coming up and before long you
could not see three feet in front of yourself. It seemed that the fish
were not biting. But we did catch another one each. It was now
about two o'clock, so I thought I would go to sleep for a while. I put
Steve's blanket down on the soil and laid on it and put George's on
top of me. Steve and George said they did not need any sleep
because they were not tired. I suppose I was asleep for about one
hour and when I woke up there was both of them asleep in their
chairs. I knew they could not keep awake for long. I went on fishing
but with no luck, then Steve woke up. We both sat down and had
something to eat and drink. We were having no more bites so Steve
and myself went to get some more wood, we built another fire and
then I woke up George. First light was now breaking and we

thought that now the fish would start biting. We changed to float fishing because it was now light and we would be able to see the float. We cast out and waited. We were now catching fish all the time but they were only bleak and gudgeon, which are only small fish. At about twelve o'clock we started to pack up because we were only catching small fish. We took the gear to the car and set off home.

Andrew Mills

Ode to the Tomato

The street
drowns in tomatoes:
noon,
summer,
light
breaks
in two
tomato
halves,
and the streets
run
with juice.
In December
the tomato
cuts loose,
invades
kitchens,
takes over lunches,
settles
at rest
on sideboards,
with the glasses,
butter dishes,
blue salt-cellars.
It has
its own radiance,
a goodly majesty.
Too bad we must
assassinate:
a knife
plunged
into its living pulp,
red
viscera,
a fresh,
deep,
inexhaustible
sun
floods the salads
of Chile,
beds cheerfully
with the blonde onion,
and to celebrate
oil
the filial essence

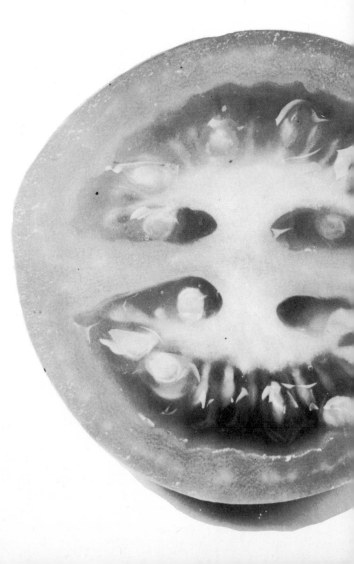

of the olive tree
let itself fall
over its gaping hemispheres,
the pimento
adds
its fragrance,
salt its magnetism –
we have the day's
wedding:
parsley
flaunts
its little flags,
potatoes
thump to a boil,
the roasts
beat
down the door
with their aromas:
it's time!
let's go!
and upon
the table,
belted by summer,
tomatoes,
stars of the earth,
stars multiplied
and fertile
show off
their convolutions,
canals
and plenitudes
and the abundance
boneless,
without husk,
or scale or thorn,
grant us
the festival
of ardent colour
and all-embracing freshness.

Pablo Neruda
*Translated from the Spanish
by Nathaniel Tarn*

Dog

The dog trots freely in the street
and sees reality
and the things he sees
are bigger than himself
and the things he sees
are his reality
Drunks in doorways
Moons on trees
The dog trots freely thru the street
and the things he sees
are smaller than himself
Fish on newsprint
Ants in holes
Chickens in Chinatown windows
their heads a block away
The dog trots freely in the street
and the things he smells
smell something like himself

The dog trots freely in the street
past puddles and babies
cats and cigars
poolrooms and policemen
He doesn't hate cops
He merely has no use for them
and he goes past them
and past the dead cows hung up whole
in front of the San Francisco Meat Market
He would rather eat a tender cow
than a tough policeman
though either might do . . .
The dog trots freely in the street
and has his own dog's life to live
and to think upon
and to reflect upon
touching and tasting and testing everything
investigating everything
without benefit of perjury
a real realist
with a real tale to tell
and a real tail to tell it with
a real live
              barking
                    democratic dog

engaged in real
               free enterprise
with something to say
               about ontology
something to say
               about reality
               and how to see it
               and how to hear it
with his head cocked sideways
               at street corners
as if he was just about to have
               his picture taken
               for Victor Records
listening for
               His Master's Voice
and looking
               like a living question mark
               into the
               great gramophone
with its wondrous hollow horn
               of puzzling existence
               which always seems
just about to spout forth
               some Victorious answer
               to everything

Lawrence Ferlinghetti

Man in the Dark

Man in the dark
peeing against a wall in the rain
holding an umbrella over him
pleased with everything wet.

John Tagliabue

My Long Woollen Underwear

My
long
woollen
under
wear
follow
me
around
a
little
loosely
like
some
inexact
but
pleasing
thought

John Tagliabue

Reckless

Last night I was reckless –
didn't brush my teeth
and went to bed tasting
my dinner all night

And it tasted good.

Pete Brown

When I Went Out

When I went out
In the Spring Meadows
To gather violets
I enjoyed myself
So much that I stayed all night.

Akahito
Translated from the Japanese by Kenneth Rexroth

Sunday

Up early while everyone sleeps,
I wander through the house,
pondering the eloquence
of vacant furniture, listening
to birdsong peeling
the cover off the day.

I think everyone I know
is sleeping now. Sidewalks
are cool, waiting for
roller skates and wagons.
Skate keys are covered
with dew; bicycles look
broken, abandoned on the lawns –
no balance left in them,
awkward as wounded
animals. I am the last
man and this is my
last day; I can't think
of anything to do. Somewhere
over my shoulder a jet
explores a crease
in the cloudy sky;
I sit on the porch
waiting for things to happen.

O fat god of Sunday
and chocolate bars, watcher
over picnics and visits to the zoo,
will anyone wake up today?

Vern Rutsala

Secondnight in
New York City after 3 years

I was happy I was bubbly drunk
The street was dark
I waved to a young policeman
He smiled
I went up to him and like a flood of gold
Told him all about my prison youth
About how noble and great some convicts were
And about how I just returned from Europe
Which wasn't half as enlightening as prison
And he listened attentively I told no lie
Everything was truth and humor
He laughed
He laughed
And it made me so happy I said :
'Absolve it all, kiss me !'
'No no no no !' he said
and hurried away.

Gregory Corso

Few

Alone tired halfdrunk hopeful
I staggered into the bogs
at Green Park Station
and found 30 written on the wall

Appalled I lurched out
into the windy blaring neon Piccadilly night
thinking surely,
Surely there must be more of us than that . . .

Pete Brown

The Street-Cleaner with his
Eighteenth-Century Muck Cart

must have been used for 'bring out your dead'
giant mexican-hat wheels, no handles,
to be pushed along after the brush has done its job
and the wheels make the same sounds on the cobbles,
an employee at the corporation yard, but smiles,
a flatcap, a boiler suit, but still that look
of the eighteenth century
you would say an idiot smile though I say old turnips and blobs
in his cart with straw and broken glass are typical.
He is his own man.

Tom Pickard

Camp Life

'Well, don't mope, lads,' he said. 'We'll live through it, even in this power-station. Get going, the mortar-mixers. Don't wait for the hooter.'

That's what a team is. A guard can't get people to budge even in working hours, but a team-leader can tell his men to get on with the job even during the break, and they'll do it. Because he's the one who feeds them. And he'd never make them work for nothing.

'Eh!' Pavlo sprang to his feet. He was young, his blood was fresh, camp life hadn't as yet worn him out. His face had been fattened on Ukranian dumplings. 'If you're going to lay blocks, I'll make the mortar for you myself. We'll see who's working the harder. Hey, where's the longest spade?'

That's what a team-leader is too. Pavlo had been a forest sniper, he'd even been on night raids. Try and make *him* break his back in a camp! But to work for the team-leader – that was different.

Shukhov and Kilgas came out on to the second storey. They heard Senka creaking up the ramp behind them. So he'd guessed, the deaf 'un.

Only a start had been made with laying the blocks on the second-storey walls. Three rows all round, a bit higher here and there. That was when the laying went fastest. From the knee to the chest, without the help of a platform.

All the platforms and trestles that had been there had been pilfered by the zeks: some had been carried off to other buildings, some had been burned. Anything to prevent another team getting them. But now everything had to be done in good order. Tomorrow they must nail some trestles together, otherwise the work would be held up.

You could see a long way from up there: the whole snow-clad, deserted expanse of the site (the zeks were hiding away, warming up before the dinner-break ended), the dark watch-towers and the sharp-tipped poles for the barbed wire. You couldn't see the wire itself except when you looked into the sun. The sun was very bright, it made you blink.

And also, not far away, you could see the mobile electro-station smoking away, blackening the sky. And wheezing, too. It always made that hoarse, sickly noise before it hooted. There it went. So they hadn't, after all, cut too much off the dinner-break.

'Hey, stakhanovite! Hurry up with that plumb,' Kilgas shouted.

'Look how much ice you've left on your wall! See if you can manage to chip it off before evening,' Shukhov said derisively. '*You* needn't have brought your trowel up with you!'

56

They'd intended to start with the walls they'd been allocated before dinner, but Tiurin called from below:

'Hey, lads! We'll work in pairs, so that the mortar doesn't freeze in the hods. You take Senka with you on your wall, and I'll work with Kilgas. But to start with, you stand in for me, Gopchik, and clean up Kilgas's wall.'

Shukhov and Kilgas looked at one another. Correct. Quicker that way.

They grabbed their axes.

And now Shukhov was no longer seeing that distant view where sun gleamed on snow. He was no longer seeing the prisoners as they wandered from the warming-up places all over the site, some to hack away at the pits they hadn't finished that morning, some to fix the mesh reinforcement, some to erect trusses in the work-shops. Shukhov was seeing only his wall – from the junction where the blocks rose in steps, higher than his waist, to where it met Kilgas's. He showed Senka where to remove ice and chopped at it zealously himself with the back and blade of his axe, so that splinters of ice flew all about and into his face. He worked with zest, but his thoughts were elsewhere. His thoughts and his eyes were feeling their way under the ice to the wall itself, the outer façade of the power-station, two blocks thick. At the spot he was working on, the wall had previously been laid by some mason who was either incompetent or had scamped the job. But now Shukhov tackled the wall as if it was his own handiwork. There, he saw, was a cavity that couldn't be levelled up in one row: he'd have to do it in three, adding a little more mortar each time. And here the outer wall bellied a bit – it would take two rows to straighten that. He divided the wall mentally into the place where he would lay blocks, starting at the point where they rose in steps, and the place where Senka was working, on the right, up to Kilgas's section. There in the corner, he reckoned, Kilgas wouldn't hold back, he would lay a few blocks for Senka, to make things easier for him. And, while they were pottering about in the corner, Shukhov would forge ahead and have the wall built, so that this pair wouldn't be behindhand. He noted how many blocks he'd require for each of the places. And the moment the carriers brought the blocks up he shouted at Alyosha:

'Bring 'em to me. Put 'em here. And here.'

Senka had finished chipping off the ice, and Shukhov picked up a wire brush, gripped it in both hands, and went along the wall, swishing it – to and fro, to and fro – cleaning up the top row, especially the joints, till only a snowy film was left on it.

Tiurin climbed up and, while Shukhov was still busy with his brush, fixed up a levelling-rod in the corner. Shukhov and Kilgas had already placed theirs on the edges of their walls.

'Hey,' called Pavlo from below. 'Anyone alive up there? Take the mortar.'

Shukhov broke into a sweat: he hadn't stretched his string over the blocks yet. He was hard pressed. He decided to stretch it for three rows at once, and make the necessary allowance. He decided also to take over a little of the outer wall from Senka and give him some of the inside instead; things would be easier for him that way.

Stretching his string along the top edge, he explained to Senka, with mouthings and gestures, where he was to work. Senka understood, for all his deafness. He bit his lips and glanced aside with a nod at Tiurin's wall. 'Shall we make it hot for him?' his look said. 'We shan't trail behind.' He laughed.

Now the mortar was being brought up the ramp. Tiurin decided not to have any of it dumped beside the masons – it would only freeze while being shifted on to the hods. The men were to put down their barrows: the masons would take the mortar straight from them and get on with the laying. Meanwhile the carriers, not to waste time, would shift on the blocks that other prisoners were heaving up from below. Directly the mortar had been scooped up from one pair of barrows, another pair would be coming and the first would go down. At the stove in the mortar-shop, the carriers would thaw out any mortar that had frozen to their barrows – and themselves, too, while they were at it.

The barrows came up two at a time – one for Kilgas's wall, one for Shukhov's. The mortar steamed in the frost but held no real warmth in it. You slapped it on the wall with your trowel and if you dawdled it would freeze: and then you'd have to hit it with the side of a hammer – you couldn't scrape it off with a trowel. And if you laid a block a bit out of true, it would immediately freeze too and set crooked: then you'd need the back of your axe to knock it off and chip away the mortar.

But Shukhov made no mistakes. The blocks varied. If any had chipped corners or broken edges or lumps on their sides, he noticed it at once and saw which way up to lay them and where they would fit best on the wall.

Here was one. Shukhov took up some of the steaming mortar on his trowel and chucked it into the appropriate place, with his mind on the joint below (this would have to be just at the middle of the block he was going to lay). He chucked on just enough mortar to go under the one block. Then he snatched it from the pile – carefully though, so as not to tear his mittens, for with blocks you can do that in no time. He smoothed the mortar with his trowel and then – down with the block! And without losing a moment he levelled it, patting it with the side of the trowel – it wasn't lying quite trim – so that the wall should be truly in line and the block lie level both lengthwise and across. The mortar was already freezing.

Now if some mortar had oozed out to the side, you had to chop it off as quickly as possible with the edge of your trowel and fling it over the wall (in summer it would go under the next brick, but now that was impossible). Next you took another look at the joint below, for there were times when the block had partially crumbled. In that event, you slapped in some extra mortar where the defect was, and you didn't lay the block flat – you slid it from side to side, squeezing out the extra mortar between it and its neighbour. An eye on the plumb. An eye on the surface. Set. Next.

The work went with a swing. Once two rows were laid and the old faults levelled up it would go quite smoothly. But now was the time to keep your eyes skinned.

Shukhov forged ahead; he pressed along the outside wall to meet Senka. Senka had parted with Tiurin in the corner and was now working along the wall to meet him.

Shukhov winked at the mortar-carriers. Bring it up, bring it up. Steady now. Smart's the word. He was working so fast he hadn't time to wipe his nose.

He and Senka met and began to scoop out of the same mortar-hod. It didn't take them long to scrape it to the bottom.

'Mortar!' Shukhov shouted over the wall.

'Coming up!' shouted Pavlo.

Another load arrived. They emptied that one too – all the liquid mortar in it, anyhow. The rest had already frozen to the sides. Scrape it off yourselves! If you don't it's you who'll be taking it up and down again. Off you go! Next!

And now Shukhov and the other masons felt the cold no longer. Thanks to the urgent work, the first wave of heat had come over them – when you feel wet under your coat, under your jacket, under your shirt and your vest. But they didn't stop for a moment: they hurried on with the laying. And after about an hour they had their second flush of heat, the one that dries up the sweat. Their feet didn't feel cold, that was the main thing. Nothing else mattered.

Alexander Solzhenitsyn *One Day in the Life of Ivan Denisovich Translated from the Russian by Ralph Parker*

Morning Sunshine From a Prison Diary

The morning sunshine penetrates into the prison,
Sweeping away the smoke and burning away the mist.
The breath of life fills the whole universe,
And smiles light up the faces of all the prisoners.

Ho Chi Minh *The Prison Diary of Ho Chi Minh*
Translated from the Vietnamese by Aileen Palmer

The Daylight Hours (Song for Dole Wallas)

A hev gorra bairn
an a hev gorra wife
an a cannit see me bairn or wife
workin in the night,

So go way Mr Doleman
av got somethin else ti do
than spen me daylight hours
workin for you.

Yes aa am a song bird
an a song bird mustsing
an you, oh Mr Doleman
you'll not clip me wings.

So go way Mr Doleman
av gotsomethin elseti do
than spen me daylight hours
workin for you.

Grab ya job an ram it
in ya stupid gob
ad ratha gan ti prison
than de ya stinkin job.

So go way Mr Doleman
av gotsomethin elseti do
than spen me daylight hours
workin for you.

An if a gan ti prison
the world will git ti na
the walls of a prison
isin strang enuff for wa.

So grab ya job an ram it
in ya stupid gob
ad rather gan ti prison
than de ya stinkin job.

Tom Pickard

On the Dole

Frankly, I hate work. Of course I could also say with equal truth that I love work; that it is a supremely interesting activity; that it is often fascinating; that I wish I didn't have to do it; that I wish I had a job at which I could earn a decent wage. That makes six subjective statements about work and all of them are true for me.

Have a brief look at a day in my life on the dole, which, except for slight unsubtle variations, is much the same as any other day.

Up at 7.15 a.m., a smoke and a cuppa, the fire lit, the kids downstairs. See they're washed, given their bit of breakfast, properly turned out, packed off to school. Another cuppa, another smoke, switch on Housewives' Choice, relax, reflect a little on this and that, perhaps play myself a hand at bridge and after about an hour of this lot switch off Housewives' Choice. Get washed, dressed, take dog for a walk by way of the railway line and along by the pit where I pick up whatever bits of coal I can find and put them in a small sack carried for that purpose. (Business with pleasure, you see.)

Back to the house, dump coal, tell dog to be good, then off down the road to the Miners' Institute where I read the *Express*, *Morning Star*, *Scotsman*, *Guardian*, and, if it happens to be a Tuesday, change my library books, not to mention frequent involvement in the numerous and usually heated discussions that take place on all sorts of topics in the reading room any morning in the week.

After leaving the Institute I do my shopping, then back up the road, fix fire, brew another cuppa, this time with a slice of bread and marg (my usual midday repast), another smoke, then start in on the household chores. When the dishes are washed, beds made, etc., down in the chair for a bit of a doze which lasts about half an hour, then it's time to think about getting the kids' tea ready as they will soon be home.

When that's done and they've been fed, there's dinner to fix for self and wife – who, by the way, is earning a welcome shilling or two at the potato harvesting as I write this – and then, after we've eaten, got selves and dishes washed, it's down in front of the telly for the remainder of the night, except, round about 9 o'clock, for another short walk for the dog.

Coming on bedtime finds wife sound asleep in her chair worn out after her day in the fields; myself bleary-eyed and very often depressed by some of the stuff I've been looking at on the box. Soon now the missus will be pushing off to bed where she likes to read a bit, and I take in perhaps the last hour by the dying fire in the company of James Boswell or some such.

Hectic, isn't it! Lovely life if you happen to be a turnip. But I am not a turnip, mate. I am a thoughtful, sensitive, widely-read man, with cultivated tastes in music and the various arts of disputation.

Am I filled with bitterness? Yes indeed! Do I tend to be anarchistic in outlook? Unquestionably! Why am I like this? Is it natural with me, or does environmental conditioning account for most of it? The short answer is, of course, because I am such a bloody pointless waste of a good citizen.

This does not mean that I think I'm unique in the sense that I have a greater potential than anyone else and that most of it is going down the drain because of the short-sightedness of others. Nor does it mean, by the conventional standards of measurement, that I am not a good citizen now. What I am trying to get across is that whatever is possible in me, in all of us, never really gets the chance to be fully realized. The reciprocal good which all might do for each other to make life a richer, fuller, more satisfying experience is hamstrung from the outset because of the nature of the society we live in.

Anonymous *Quoted in* Work, *edited by Ronald Fraser*

Driving the Bus

The alarm clangs out – it's 3.30 a.m. Jesus! It'll wake the whole street up; they are probably turning over for their second sleep. I roll out of bed – time was when I sprang out. That was a long time ago. Rising at this hour every other week for forty years tends to become irksome and inconvenient – quite apart from its effect on your gastric juices! Forty years of catching the 8.10 a.m. every morning of my life, however, would have driven me up the wall.

The sharp tingling air of the early morning made me wish that I had put another woolly on.

A brisk walk down to the 'Bell' just in time for the first bus to Liverpool Street. After a short walk to the garage I have regained some of the warmth of the bed I left an hour or so earlier.

Signing on – we don't clock on – with five minutes to spare as against the ten minutes we are allowed before the bus is due to leave the garage. I find my bus and am out of the garage at 5.15 a.m. sharp.

Among my first passengers will be the early-morning workers from two of London's great markets – Spitalfields Fruit and Billingsgate Fish Markets.

The great majority of my first passengers, however, will be part of that vast army of women who flock in from the working-class areas on the fringe of the City of London to clean, wash and scrub the mountains of office blocks, banks and counting houses within the golden square mile.

Except for a handful of market lorries, the road is yours at this time of the morning, and you can look around and let your thoughts wander – not too much though, mate!

Among my early thoughts is one which has been with me over the years; what stories might be written about these hundreds of working-class women, old and middle-aged, who, hours before the majority of Londoners have left their beds, can be seen in the mean streets of Bermondsey, Shoreditch and Bethnal Green, waiting for the earliest buses to take them into those rich streets and offices where rent, interest and profit are determined! What circumstances compelled them to take up this work? A widow perhaps, of the 1914 or the last war? Married early, left with a family to keep, no special skills, but with a job that enables them to get back home having finished their morning scrubbing in time to get the children, or perhaps the grandchildren, off to school . . . .

We pass over London Bridge, at this early hour with few cars and fewer people (what a difference there will be on our return journey), and glance down at the Pool and across to Tower Bridge. Because it's early and passengers are few and far between, it's possible to take a second look across the bridge to the Tower of London – a great grey mass in the early light – and let your thoughts stray. The weather-stained walls and ramparts, the old guns with their campaign dates – all outstripped and replaced by the modern instruments of war, nuclear arms. Then through Tooley Street and the enormous dark and dirty warehouses, silent now as will be the Surrey Commercial Dock when I pass it within the next five minutes. On my return journey, however, I will be bringing many dockers to both. These areas will then be alive with lorries and men waiting for the 'call' to load and unload.

Within the next hour we will be bowling along the roads of Kent and, because I will probably still be with my early morning dreams, I will stop automatically at a request stop, the only thing in sight a cow or two in the fields. My conductor, who knows me well and has worked with me for years (his favourite lecture to the younger members in the garage is how he kept his wife and eight kids during the many unofficial and official strikes he took part in and how they lived on the quite inadequate strike pay of those days), will come round to the front of the bus and after looking up and down the road for the passenger who wasn't there and for whom I had stopped will ask 'Where were you then?' Knowing him, I will smile sheepishly, but offer no reply.

We are at the end of the journey – with a bit of luck we might manage a cup of tea if the cafés are open. . . .

We will talk – and it's more than likely that we will talk about the job, the public, our passengers, the bus, the bell, the stops . . . .

We will probably ask each other questions – 'Did you see that old lady – did she think I was a thought reader? She didn't put her hand up for me to stop till I was almost past her!'

'Did you see the way that driver cut me up? Good job for him that years of driving have made me hope for better things in life.'

'Did you notice that old boy? He was the third one that gave me a ten-bob note for a tanner fare in about as many minutes – lucky for him I'm not bad-tempered!'

A peculiar feature about life and work on buses is the way in which the crews are forever discussing the job; its interest; its humour; drawbacks, strain, public relationships, etc. They never tire of regaling each other with their experience on the road or on the bus.

Anonymous *Quoted in* Work, *edited by Ronald Fraser*

Flying a Spitfire

And we learned, finally, to fly the Spitfire.

I faced the prospect with some trepidation. Here for the first time was a machine in which there was no chance of making a dual circuit as a preliminary. I must solo right off, and in the fastest machine in the world.

One of the Squadron took me up for a couple of trips in a Miles Master, the British trainer most similar to a Spitfire in characteristics.

I was put through half an hour's instrument flying under the hood in a Harvard, and then I was ready. At least I hoped I was ready. Kilmartin, a slight dark-haired Irishman in charge of our Flight, said: 'Get your parachute and climb in. I'll just show you the cockpit before you go off.'

He sauntered over to the machine, and I found myself memorizing every detail of his appearance with the clearness of a condemned man on his way to the scaffold – the chin sunk into the folds of a polo sweater, the leather pads on the elbows, and the string-darned hole in the seat of the pants. He caught my look of anxiety and grinned.

'Don't worry; you'll be surprised how easy she is to handle.'

I hoped so.

The Spitfires stood in two lines outside 'A' Flight pilots' room. The dull grey-brown of the camouflage could not conceal the clear-cut beauty, the wicked simplicity of their lines. I hooked up my parachute and climbed awkwardly into the low cockpit. I noticed how small was my field of vision. Kilmartin swung himself on to a wing and started to run through the instruments. I was conscious of his voice, but heard nothing of what he said. I was to fly a Spitfire. It was what I had most wanted through all the long dreary months of training. If I could fly a Spitfire, it would be worth it. Well, I was about to achieve my ambition and felt nothing. I was numb, neither exhilarated nor scared. I notice the white enamel undercarriage handle. 'Like a lavatory plug,' I thought.

'What did you say?'

Kilmartin was looking at me and I realized I had spoken aloud. I pulled myself together.

'Have you got all that?' he asked.

'Yes, sir.'

'Well, off you go then. About four circuits and bumps. Good luck!'

He climbed down.

I taxied slowly across the field, remembering suddenly what I had been told: that the Spitfire's prop was long and that it was therefore inadvisable to push the stick too far forward when taking off; that

the Spitfire was not a Lysander and that any hard application of the brake when landing would result in a somersault and immediate transfer to a 'Battle' squadron. Because of the Battle's lack of power and small armament this was regarded by everyone as the ultimate disgrace.

I ran quickly through my cockpit drill, swung the nose into wind, and took off. I had been flying automatically for several minutes before it dawned on me that I was actually in the air, undercarriage retracted and half-way round the circuit without incident. I turned into wind and hauled up on my seat, at the same time pushing back the hood. I came in low, cut the engine just over the boundary hedge, and floated down on all three points. I took off again. Three more times I came round for a perfect landing. It was too easy. I waited across wind for a minute and watched with satisfaction several machines bounce badly as they came in. Then I taxied rapidly back to the hangars and climbed out nonchalantly. Noel, who had not yet sooled, met me.

'How was it?' he said.

I made a circle of approval with my thumb and forefinger.

'Money for old rope,' I said.

I didn't make another good landing for a week.

The flight immediately following our first solo was an hour's aerobatics. I climbed up to 12,000 feet before attempting even a slow roll.

Kilmartin had said, 'See if you can make her talk.' That meant the whole bag of tricks, and I wanted ample room for mistakes and possible blacking out. With one or two very sharp movements on the stick I blacked myself out for a few seconds, but the machine was sweeter to handle than any other that I had flown. I put it through every manoeuvre that I knew of and it responded beautifully. I ended with two flick rolls and turned back for home. I was filled with a sudden exhilarating confidence. I could fly a Spitfire; in any position I was its master. It remained to be seen whether I could fight in one.

Richard Hillary *The Last Enemy*

The Collector

The village, when we reached it, proved to be a large, straggling one with a curious dead air about it. Even the houses, constructed as usual with the off-cuts from tree-trunks, had an ill-kempt, dirty look. Everything looked scruffy and depressed. But everyone appeared to know Coco, for when we inquired in the local bar where he lived, a forest of hands directed us and everyone smiled and said, 'Ah, yes, Coco,' as if they were referring to the village idiot.

Following directions we found his house easily enough. It would have been very noticeable anyway, for in comparison to the rest of the village, it gleamed like a gem. It had been carefully whitewashed, so that it shone; its front garden was neatly tended and, incredibly, a real gravel path, neatly raked, led up to the house. I decided that if this was the house of the village idiot, then I very much wanted to meet him. In response to our clapping a slight, dark woman appeared, who looked as though she might be Italian. She admitted to being Coco's wife, but said that he was not at home: he worked during the day at the local saw-mill, which we could hear humming in the distance like all the bees in the universe having a conference. Luna explained my mission and the wife's face lighted up.

'Oh,' she said, 'I will send one of the children to fetch him. He would never forgive me if he missed meeting you. Please come round to the back and wait . . . he will come in a few moments.'

The garden at the back of the house was as well tended as the front, and, to my surprise, contained two well-constructed and spacious aviaries. I peered into them hopefully, but they were both empty. We did not have to wait long for Coco's appearance. He appeared from the path leading to the saw-mill at a brisk trot, and arrived, breathing deeply, in front of us and doffed his straw hat. He was a short, well-built man with coal-black curly hair and (unusual in Argentina) a thick black beard and moustache, carefully trimmed. His eyes were dark, and shone with eagerness as he held out a well-shaped brown hand to Luna and myself.

'Welcome, welcome,' he said, 'you must excuse, please, my English . . . she is not good for I have no chance to practise.'

The fact that he could speak English at all amazed me.

'You have no idea what this means to me,' he said eagerly, wringing my hand, 'to speak with someone who has an interest in Nature . . . if my wife had not called me I would never have forgiven her. . . . I could not believe it when my son told me . . . an Englishman to see me, and about animals, too.'

He smiled at me, his face still slightly awe-stricken at this miracle that had happened. One would have thought that I had come to offer him the Presidency of Argentina. I was so overwhelmed at being greeted like a newly descended angel that I was almost at a loss for words.

'Well,' said Luna, having obviously decided that he had done his job by bringing one lunatic in contact with another, 'I will go and do my work and see you later.'

He drifted off, humming to himself, while Coco seized my arm gently, as though it were a butterfly's wing that he might damage, and urged me up the steps and into the living-room of his house. Here his wife had produced wonderful lemonade from fresh lemons, heavily sweetened, and we sat at the table and drank this while Coco talked. He spoke quietly, stumbling occasionally in his English and saying a sentence in Spanish when he realized I knew enough of the language to follow. It was an extraordinary experience, like listening to a man who had been dumb for years suddenly recover the power of speech. He had been living for so long in a world of his own, for neither his wife, children nor anyone in the fly-blown village could understand his interests. To him I was the incredible answer to a prayer, a man who could understand what he meant when he said a bird was beautiful, or an animal was interesting, someone, in fact, who could speak this language that had so long been locked up inside him, which no one around him comprehended. All the time he spoke he watched me with an embarrassing expression, a mixture of awe and fear – awe that I should be there at all, and fear that I might suddenly disappear like a mirage.

'It is the birds that I am particularly studying,' he said, 'I know the birds of Argentina are catalogued, but who knows anything about them? Who knows their courtship displays, their type of nests, how many eggs they lay, how many broods they have, if they migrate? Nothing is known of this, and this is the problem. In this field I am trying to help, as well as I can.'

'This is the problem all over the world,' I said, 'we know what creatures exist – or most of them – but we know nothing of their private lives.'

'Would you like to see the place where I work? I call it my study,' he explained deprecatingly, 'it is very small, but all I can afford. . . .'

'I would love to see it,' I said.

Eagerly he led me outside to where a sort of miniature wing had been built on to the side of the house. The door that led into this was heavily padlocked. As he pulled a key from his pocket to open this he smiled at me.

'I let no one in here,' he explained simply, 'they do not understand.' Up until then I had been greatly impressed with Coco, and with his obvious enthusiasm for animal life. But now, being led into his study, I was more than impressed. I was speechless.

His study was about eight feet long and six feet wide. In one corner was a cabinet which housed, as he showed me, his collection of bird and small mammal skins, and various birds' eggs. Then there was a long low bench on which he did his skinning, and nearby a rough bookcase containing some fourteen volumes on natural history, some in Spanish, some in English. Under one small window stood an easel, and on it the half-finished water colour of a bird, whose corpse lay on a box.

'Did you do that?' I asked incredulously.

'Yes,' he said shyly, 'you see, I could not afford a camera, and this was the only way to record their plumage.'

I gazed at the half-finished picture. It was beautifully done, with a fineness of line and colouring that was amazing. I say amazing because the drawing and painting of birds is one of the most difficult of subjects in the whole natural-history field. Here was work that was almost up to the standards of some of the best modern bird painters I had seen. You could see that it was the work of an untrained person, but it was done with meticulous accuracy and love, and the bird glowed on the page. I had the dead specimen in my hand to compare the painting with, and I could see that this painting was far better than a lot I had seen published in bird books.

He pulled out a great folder and showed me his other work. He had some forty paintings of birds, generally in pairs if there was any sexual difference in the plumage, and they were all as good as the first one I had seen.

'But these are terribly good,' I said, 'you must do something with them.'

'Do you think so?' he inquired doubtfully, peering at the paintings. 'I have sent some to the man in charge of the Museum at Cordoba, and he liked them. He said we should have a small book printed when I have enough of them, but this I think is doubtful, for you know how costly a production would be.'

'Well I know the people in charge of the Museum at Buenos Aires,' I said. 'I will speak to them about you. I don't guarantee anything, but they might be able to help.'

'That would be wonderful,' he said, his eyes shining.

'Tell me,' I said, 'do you like your work here in the saw-mill?'

'Like it?' he repeated incredulously, 'like it? Senor, it is soul-destroying. But it provides me with enough to live on, and by careful saving I have enough left over to buy paints. Also I am saving to buy a small cine-camera, for however skilful you are as a painter there are certain things that birds do which can only be captured on film. But these cine-cameras are very expensive, and I am afraid it will be a long time before I can afford it.'

He talked on for an hour or so, quickly, enthusiastically, telling me what he had accomplished and what he hoped to do. I had to keep reminding myself that this was a man – a peasant, if you prefer the term – who worked in a saw-mill and lived in a house which, though spotless, no so-called worker in England would be seen dead in. To have discovered Coco in the outskirts of Buenos Aires would not have been, perhaps, so incredible, but to find him here in this remote, unlikely spot, was like suddenly coming across a unicorn in the middle of Piccadilly.

Gerald Durrell *The Whispering Land*

The Blondin of Dublin

And still the years kept rolling on, and uneventfully enough, thank God. I was now about eleven, the brother sixteen and convinced he was a fully grown man.

One day in spring about half-three I was trudging wearily home from school at Synge Street. I was on the remote, or canal side of the roadway near home. I happened to glance up at the house when about fifty yards away and, turned to cold stone, stopped dead in my tracks. My heart thumped wildly against my ribs and my eyes fell to the ground. I blessed myself. Timidly I looked up again. Yes!

To the left of the house entrance and perhaps fifteen yards from it a tallish tree stood in the front garden. Head and shoulders above the tree but not quite near it was the brother. I stared at the apparition in the manner fascinated animals are reputed to stare at deadly snakes about to strike. He began waving his arms in a sickening way, and the next prospect I had of him was his back. He was returning towards the house *and he was walking on air*! Now thoroughly scared, I thought of Another who had walked on water. I again looked away helplessly, and after a little time painfully stumbled into the house. I must have looked very pale but went in and said nothing.

Mr Collopy was not in his usual chair at the range. Annie – we had now learned to drop the 'Miss' – placed potatoes and a big plate of stew before me. . . .

I finished with a cup of tea, then casually left the kitchen and went upstairs, my heart again making its excitement known. I entered the bedroom.

The brother, his back to me, was bending over a table examining some small metal objects. He looked up and nodded abstractedly.

'Do you mind,' I said nervously, 'do you mind answering a question?'

'What question? I have got a great bit of gear here.'

'Listen to the question. When I was coming in a while back, did I see you walking on the air?'

He turned again to stare at me and then laughed loudly.

'Well, by damn,' he chuckled, 'I suppose you did, in a manner of speaking.'

'What do you mean?'

'Your question is interesting. Did it look well?'

'If you want to know, it looked unnatural and if you are taking advantage of a power not of God, if you are dealing in godless things of darkness, I would strongly advise you to see Father Fahrt, because these things will lead to no good.'

Here he sniggered.

'Have a look out of the window,' he said.

I went and did so very gingerly. Between the sill and a stout branch near the top of the tree stretched a very taut wire, which I now saw came in at the base of the closed window and was anchored with some tightening device to the leg of the bed, which was in against the wall.

'My God Almighty!' I exclaimed.

'Isn't it good?'

'A bloody wire-walker, by cripes!'

'I got the stuff from Jem out of the Queen's. There's nothing at all to it. If I rigged the wire across this room tomorrow and only a foot from the floor, you'd walk it yourself with very little practice. What's the difference? What's the difference if you're an inch or a mile up? The only trouble is what they call psychological. It's a new word but I know what it means. The balancing part of it is child's play, and the trick is to put all idea of height out of your mind. It *looks* dangerous, of course, but there's money in that sort of danger. Safe danger.'

'What happens if you fall and break your neck?'

'Did you ever hear of Blondin? He died in his bed at the age of seventy-three, and fifty years ago he walked on a wire across Niagara Falls, one hundred and sixty feet above the roaring water. And several times – carrying a man on his back, stopping to fry eggs, a great man altogether. And didn't he appear once in Belfast?'

'I think you are going off your head.'

'I'm going to make money, for I have . . . certain schemes, certain very important schemes. Look what I have here. A printing machine. I got it from one of the lads at Westland Row, who stole it from his uncle. It's simple to operate, though it's old.'

But I could not detach my mind from that wire.

'So you're to be the Blondin of Dublin?'

'Well, why not?'

'Niagara is too far away, of course. I suppose you'll sling a wire over the Liffey?'

He started, threw down some metal thing, and turned to me wide-eyed.

'Well, sweet God,' he said, 'you have certainly said something. *You have certainly said something.* Sling a wire over the Liffey? The Masked Daredevil from Mount Street! There's a fortune there – *a fortune!* Lord save us, why didn't I think of it?'

'I was only joking, for goodness' sake.'

'*Joking?* I hope you'll keep on joking like that. I'll see Father Fahrt about this.'

'To bless you before you risk your life?'

'Balls! I'll need an organizer, a manager. Father Fahrt knows a lot of those young teachers and I'll get him to put me on to one of them. They're a sporty crowd. Do you remember Frank Corkey, N.T.? He was in this house once, a spoilt Jesuit. That man would blow up the walls of Jerusalem for two quid. He'd be the very man.'

'And get sacked from his school for helping a young madman to kill himself?'

'I'll get him. You wait and see.'

That ended that day's surprising disputation. I was secretly amused at the idea of the brother getting on to Father Fahrt about organizing a walk across the Liffey on a tight-wire, with Mr Collopy sprawled in his cane armchair a few feet away listening to the appeal. I had heard of earthquakes and the devastation attending them. Here surely would be a terrible upheaval.

But once more I reckoned without the brother. Without saying a word he slipped off one day up to 35, Lower Leeson Street and saw Father Fahrt privately. He said so when he returned that evening, looking slightly daunted.

'The holy friar,' he said, 'won't hear of it. Asked did I think I was a cornerboy or had I no respect for my family. Public pranks is what he called walking the high wire. Threatened to tell ould Collopy if I didn't put the idea out of my head. Asked me to promise. I promised, of course. But I'll find Corkey on my own and we'll make a damn fine day of it, believe you me. Had I no respect for my family, ah? What family?'

'No Jesuit likes being mistaken for a Barnum,' I pointed out.

Rather bitterly he said: 'You'll hear more about this.'

I felt sure I would.

Flann O'Brien *The Hard Life*

where the giant unlocked a cellar door and showed him
gold: 'One is for the poor, the second for the King, a[nd the third]
yours.' Just then the clock struck twelve and the giant v[anished, leaving]
the boy in total darkness. Next morning the King came [and asked what]
had happened. 'My dead cousin came to see me and t[old me where a dead]
fellow showed me three treasure chests in the cellar; but [nothing could make]
me to shudder.' The King was overjoyed: 'You have sav[ed my kingdom,']
he cried, 'now you may marry my daughter.'

The young Prince loved his wife but he still complain[ed]

School Play

*(Makarenko is teaching in a school for delinquent boys in Russia.
It is known as a colony and the boys in it are referred to as colonists.)*

On Saturday things got lively around the theatre from two o'clock
onwards. If there were many characters, Butsai, assisted by Pyotr
Ivanovich, would begin making them up immediately after dinner.
From eight p.m. they could get as many as sixty people ready, and
make themselves up afterwards.

When it was a matter of getting properties for a performance the
colonists behaved more like wild beasts than human beings. If a
lamp with a blue shade was needed on the stage they would raid not
only the rooms of the staff, but the rooms of friends in town, and the
lamp with the blue shade would be sure to be forthcoming. If they
sat down to supper on the stage, the supper must be a real one,
without any evasions. This was demanded not only by the thorough-
ness of 6-P Mixed (props), but by tradition. To have supped on the
stage upon dummy dishes would have seemed to our actors
unworthy of the colony. Our kitchen, therefore, was sometimes
confronted with difficult tasks – the preparation of hors d'oeuvres
and entrées, the baking of pies and cakes. For wine we used cider.

In my prompter's box I was always in a twitter during a supper
scene: the actors at such moments became so engrossed in their
roles that they took no notice of the prompter, dragging the scene
out till nothing was left on the table. I was usually forced to speed up
a scene by such remarks as: 'That'll do! D'you hear? Stop eating!'

The actors would glance at me in astonishment, motioning with their eyes towards a half-eaten goose, and would only leave the table when, losing my temper, I would hiss 'Karabanov – get up from the table! Semyon! Say "I'm off!"'

Karabanov would hastily bolt the half-chewed mouthful of goose, and say: 'I'm off!' And in the wings, during the interval, I would get moaned at: 'Anton Semyonovich, how could you? How often does one get a chance to eat such a goose? And you wouldn't let us finish it!'

But the actors were not as a rule anxious to stay too long on the stage, where it was as cold as out of doors. In *The Riot of the Machines* Karabanov had to stay a whole hour on the stage, with nothing on but a loincloth. The performance took place in February, and, unluckily for us, the thermometer sometimes fell to thirty degrees below zero. Ekaterina Grigoryevna insisted on the performance being cancelled, assuring us that Semyon would certainly be frozen. But everything was all right – only Semyon's toes were frozen, and after the act Ekaterina Grigoryevna rubbed him with some sort of a warming mixture.

But the cold did sometimes stand in the way of our artistic development. We were giving a play called *Comrade Semivzvodny*. The scene was laid in the garden of a landowner, and there was supposed to be a statue. Six-P Mixed could find no statue, though they looked in all the town cemeteries, and they decided to do without. But when the curtain went up, to my astonishment I did see a statue – there was Shelaputin thickly powdered with chalk, and wrapped in a sheet, looking slyly down at me from a draped stool. I lowered the curtain and chivvied the statue off the stage, to the great disappointment of 6-P Mixed.

The efforts of 6-SE Mixed (sound-effects) were particularly conscientious and ingenious. We were producing Azef. Sazonov was to throw a bomb at Plehve. The bomb was to explode. Osadchy, the commander of 6-SE Mixed, declared: 'We'll make that a real explosion.' Since I was acting Plehve myself, I was more interested in this than anyone else.

'And what d'you mean by "real"?' I inquired.

'One which would blow the theatre to smithereens.'

'That's a bit too much,' I said cautiously.

'It'll be all right,' Osadchy assured me. 'It'll all come right in the end.'

Before the scene with the explosion, Osadchy showed me his preparations – in front of the wings were placed a few empty tubs, beside each tub stood a colonist with a double-barrelled gun, charged with about enough to kill an elephant. On the other side of the stage, bits of glass were strewn about the floor, a colonist with a brick posted beside each bit. On the third side, opposite the entrance to the stage, about half a dozen kids were placed with lighted candles in front of them, and bottles containing liquid of some sort in their hands.

'What's the funeral for?' I asked.

'That's the chief thing. They've got paraffin. When the time comes they'll fill their mouths with paraffin and blow it on to the candles. It'll be splendid!'

'You're mad! There might be a fire!'

'Don't worry, only take care not to get any paraffin in your eyes – if there's a fire we'll put it out.' He pointed to yet another line of colonists, at whose feet were pails full of water.

'But can paraffin be extinguished with water?' I asked. Osadchy was invulnerable, he knew all this side of the business and could explain it in the most knowing manner. 'When paraffin is blown on to the flame of a candle, it is converted into gas, and does not require extinguishing. Other objects may have to be extinguished.'

'Me, for example?'

'We'll put you out first of all.'

I submitted to my fate. If I was not burned to death I should at least be doused with cold water, and that at a temperature of nearly twenty degrees below zero! But how could I show myself up in front of the whole of 6-SE Mixed, who had spent so much energy and inventiveness on the preparations for the explosion?

When Sazonov threw the bomb I once more had the opportunity of getting into Plehve's skin, and I did not envy him. The hunting rifles were fired at the tubs, and the tubs shivered, bursting their hoops and my eardrums, the bricks descended with terrific force upon the glass, five or six mouths blew the paraffin with all the force of youthful lungs on to the candle flames, and the whole stage was suddenly converted into a suffocating, flaming mass. I could not have played my own death badly if I had wanted to, and fell down almost unconscious, beneath a deafening roar of applause and the enthusiastic yells of 6-SE Mixed. From above, black, greasy paraffin ash fell upon me. The curtain was drawn, and Osadchy helped me up, asking anxiously:

'You're not burning anywhere, are you?'

I was burning inwardly, but I said nothing about that – who knows what 6-SE Mixed had prepared for such an event!

A. S. Makarenko *The Road to Life*

Carnival

The moon's windows lit from inside, lightly steamed over.
The shadow of a hand appeared outlined on them. The hand
quietly opened the window, showed to the wrist, and threw down
a white cotton pierrot costume. For a moment the bells tinkled on the
pavement. He was startled.
He looked all around. No one. Lampstands, telegraph-poles motionless.

Hastily he threw the silver cloak over his shoulders and entered the
room, confident now, smiling, upright, they all applauded him.
Only the bells tinkling a little earlier, outside his body,
before his disguise, rang still guiltily in the road,
guiltily and treacherously at once. But he quickly realized
that only he could hear them amid all the music, light and masks.

Yannis Ritsos *Translated from the Greek by Paul Merchant*

Going to a Silent Movie

The show would have begun. As we stumbled along behind the attendant, I felt I was there surreptitiously; above our heads, a beam of white light would be shining across the hall, and dust and smoke would be dancing in it; a piano would be tinkling, violet light-bulbs would be glowing on the wall, and I would catch my breath at the varnish-like smell of a disinfectant. The smell and the fruits of that inhabited night mingled within me: I was eating the exit lights, filling myself with their acid taste. I would scrape my back against people's knees, sit on a creaking seat. My mother slipped a folded rug under my buttocks to raise me up; finally I would look at the screen and would see fluorescent chalk, and shimmering landscapes streaked with rain; it was always raining, even in bright sunshine, even inside a flat; sometimes a fiery planet would cross a baroness's drawing-room without her appearing to be surprised. I used to love that rain, that restless disquiet which tormented the wall. The pianist would strike up the overture to *Fingal's Cave* and everyone would know that the villain was about to appear: the baroness would be crazed with terror. But her handsome, dusky face would be replaced by a mauve notice: 'End of first part'. Then would come the abrupt sobering-up and the lights. Where was I? At school? In a government office? No ornaments of any kind: rows of tip-up seats which revealed their springs when pushed up, walls smeared with ochre, and a wooden floor littered with cigarette ends and spittle. Muffled voices would fill the hall, words would exist once more; the attendant would offer boiled sweets for sale and my mother would buy me some; I would put them in my mouth and I was sucking the exit lights. People would rub their eyes and everyone would realize he had neighbours.

Jean-Paul Sartre *Words*

Going to the Pictures

One Saturday morning I got up and it was raining. I got ready and washed and then my friends knocked for me.

'Do you want to go to the pictures?'

'Yes,' I said. 'What shall we see?'

'*Thoroughly Modern Millie.*'

That afternoon we all got ready to go to the pictures. We got a 63 bus to take us to the Elephant and Castle, because the pictures are just next door. There was a great big queue waiting to go in and we were at the very back. Soon we got in. The picture had already started and it was very dark in there. We had to go down some stairs to get to our seats but instead of walking down them we fell down them. Soon we were in our seats. We were all sitting there watching the film when something hit me on the head. It was an ice-cream tub. I turned round to see who it was and a little boy who was sitting two rows behind me said, 'I am very sorry. It wasn't meant to hit you. It was meant to hit the boy in front.'

'That's all right,' I said. 'But don't throw anything again.' I turned back and started watching the film. Then my friend wanted to go to the toilet and she wanted someone to go with her, so I went. She washed her face and combed her hair and we were about a quarter of an hour in there. We returned to our seats. Then I wanted something to eat so I went outside and bought a hot dog, a shilling bar of chocolate, peppermints and a drink. Then I went back to my seat. I offered the sweets to my friends but they did not want any. I soon ate and drank the lot.

After watching the film for a while we saw some girls we knew, but we did not like them so we all hid down in our seats so that they would not see us. As soon as we got up one of them shouted, 'Look who's over there.' They all came over and sat next to us. They kept on talking and I couldn't hear one bit of the film. Then it was the intermission and the lights went on. There was a lady selling ice-creams and peanuts. One of my friends got four tubs and four packets of nuts, one for each of us.

Soon the next bit of the film came on. We were still eating our ice-creams. One of my friends had gone to sleep, but we all woke her up. Some boys and girls behind us started shouting and swearing and a man with a torch came up and said, 'I am afraid I will have to ask you to go out because you are making far too much noise.'

They said, 'If we go out we will have our money back.'

'You will not.' There was a big argument and at last the man threw them out and it was much quieter.

One of my friends had her little brother with her and he started crying. He would not stop until we gave him some sweets. Soon afterwards he went to sleep. Then the film ended and it was a very good film, what I saw of it. Then we got a 63 bus home and I got in about six o'clock. It had stopped raining.

Anonymous

Holiday Camps

From behind a plastic rose bush the Camp Radio strikes up. It sings:

'Hello campers
There's a good time on the way
For wet or fine, the sun will always shine
On your good-time holiday.'

'Here's a suggestion for your morning's entertainment – meet Uncle Len in the Venetian Lounge.'

We go. It is competition time. As we enter, a few thousand bulbs, lemon and orange, light up in the ceiling.

Uncle Len is a sporty fellow who wears a brilliant blazer with the camp emblem on it. 'Well, this morning is mainly for the children. But all are welcome. We're going to have quite a number of competitions before we're finished, in fact we've got competitions going through the day. To help us out we've got various Aunties. Let's see, our chief Auntie is Auntie Meg. There she is. Isn't she a nice Auntie? Her name is Auntie Meg. Then there's our junior campers' leading Auntie, her name is Auntie Cath. Yes, Auntie Cath. But I call her matchsticks.

'Now all these Aunties have their funny little habits. Auntie Jane, for instance, collects bottle tops. Auntie Cath collects boyfriends.

'Now that man over there with the television set, he's a photographer. Why is that little girl over there standing up? What do you think, children? I think she must be like a railway engine, she's got a tender behind.

'Now what other uncles and aunties have we got? Ah, here there's a table-tennis coach, specially sent down from London, he's a coach, that's not the thing you go down to the sea in for excursions, no, it's a coach, a table-tennis coach.

'Then there's Uncle Tommy and his magic – and what else have we – ah, here is the camp padre, a big hand –'

The camp padre skips on to the stage, holding up his vestments: 'Good morning, junior campers. A few weeks ago I was browsing through the newspapers without a thought in my head. Then my eye was caught by a small news item. It mentioned that the Lotus firm has perfected a new racing car. We shall be hearing more about the Lotus racing car in the current week. And more too about the word of our Lord Jesus Christ.'

He skips off. Uncle Len says: 'That's about all, I think. Oh yes, I forgot just two more. That's Auntie Mary and Auntie Val. Auntie Mary and Auntie Val are singists. Yes they're very good singists.

'So, here we are, let's get going on the competitions. Everyone ready? All of you warmed up? Oh good. And here we've got our Walls Ice-Cream person all ready, in case any of you is a bit hot. Anyone a bit hot – anyone hot? Auntie Mary, I think we've got all these children warmed up.'

When the children leave the Venetian Ballroom we stay behind. A few minutes later it's filled once more, this time with adults.

Uncle Len is still on duty, although he now wears a more sophisticated face. He says: 'And now to introduce you to the Goldjacket in charge of whatever block you may happen to be in. First – Exeter Block.'

The Goldjacket in charge of Exeter Block leaps up on the stage. Young for so responsible a position, he seems the typical public schoolboy, gold-haired, clean-limbed. He shouts: 'Hi folks! Now, all you lucky people in Exeter Block, I want you to do this for me. When you see me, shout "Mashed Potatoes!" Well, I've been asked to say a few words about this block, well it's the best block, we all know that, the best block. I must admit it.' This statement is followed by cheers and boos.

'Now for Plymouth Block.'

The young Master of Plymouth Block sprints up on the stage: 'Well folks, Plymouth Block is the best, we all know that, it's the best, I have to admit it, the best, now whenever you see me will you please all shout like this: "Zigga Zagga Zigga Zagga. Ho! Ho! Ho!"'

Outside the Radio speaks forth through loudspeakers hidden among the roses: 'Campers may care to note that a cash Bingo Session is now in operation in the Bingo Hall.'

Jeremy Sandford *Synthetic Fun*

Wedding

'D'bloved we gath'd gether sighto' Gard'n face this con-gation join gather Man Woom Ho Mat-mony which is on'bl state stooted by Gard in times man in'cency . . .'

Mr Polly's thoughts wandered wide and far and once again something like a cold hand touched his heart, and he saw a sweet face in sunshine under the shadow of trees. Someone was nudging him. It was Johnson's finger diverting his eyes to the crucial place in the prayer book to which they had come.

'Wiltou lover, comfer, oner keeper sickness and health . . .'

'Say, "I will"!'

Mr Polly moistened his lips. 'I will' he said hoarsely.

Miriam, nearly inaudible, answered some similar demand.

Then the clergyman said: 'Who gi's Wom mad't this man?'

'Well I'm doing that,' said Mr Voules in a refreshingly full voice, and looking round the church. 'Pete arf me,' said the clergyman to Mr Polly. 'Take thee Miriam wed wife –'

'Take thee Mi'm wed wife,' said Mr Polly.

'Have hold thes dayford.'

'Have hold this day ford.'

'Beteorse, richypoo'.'

'Bet worse, richypoo' . . .'

Then came Miriam's turn.

'Lego hands,' said the clergyman, 'gothering? No! On book. So. Here! Pete arf me "Wis ring Ivy wed".' 'Wis ring Ivy wed. . . .'

So it went on, blurred and hurried, like the momentary vision of a very beautiful thing seen through the smoke of a passing train . . . .

'Now my boy,' said Mr Voules at last, gripping Mr Polly's elbow tightly, 'you've gotto sign the registry and there you are! Done!'

Before him stood Miriam, a little stiffly, the hat with a slight rake across her forehead and a kind of questioning hesitation in her face. Mr Voules urged her past him.

It was astounding. She was his wife!

And for some reason Miriam and Mrs Larkin were sobbing, and Annie was looking grave. Hadn't they after all wanted him to marry her? Because if that was the case. . . .

Outside, a crowd of half a dozen adults and about fifty children had collected, and hailed the approach of the newly-wedded couple with a faint, indeterminate cheer. All the children were holding something in little bags, and his attention was caught by the expression of vindictive concentration upon the face of a small big-eared boy in the foreground. He didn't for the moment realize what these things might import. Then he received a stinging handful of rice in the ear and a great light shone.

'Not yet, you young fool,' he heard Mr Voules saying behind him, and then a second handful spoke against his hat. . . .

And then came a great wedging and squeezing and crowding into the little room. Nearly everyone was hungry, and eyes brightened at the sight of the pie, and the ham, and the convivial array of bottles. 'Sit down, everyone,' cried Mr Voules. 'Leaning against anything counts as sitting, and makes it easier to shake down the grub!'

The two friends from Miriam's place of business came into the room among the first, and then wedged themselves so hopelessly against Johnson in an attempt to get out again to take off their things upstairs, that they abandoned the attempt. Amid the struggle, Mr Polly saw Uncle Pentstemon relieve himself of his parcel by giving it to the bride.

'Here!' he said, and handed it to her. 'Weddin' present,' he exclaimed, and added with a confidential chuckle, 'I never thought I'd 'ave to give one – ever.'

'Who says steak-and-kidney pie?' bawled Mr Voules. 'Who says steak-and-kidney pie? You 'ave a drop of old Tommy, Martha. That's what you want to steady you down. . . .

'Sit down, everyone, and don't all speak at once. Who says steak-and-kidney pie?'

'Vociferations,' whispered Mr Polly. 'Convivial vociferations.'

'Bit of 'am withit,' shouted Mr Voules, poising a slice of ham on his knife. 'Anyone 'ave a bit of 'am with it? Won't that little man of yours, Mrs Punt – won't 'e 'ave a bit of 'am? And now, ladies and gentlemen,' said Mr Voules, still standing and dominating the crammed roomful, 'now you got your plates filled, and something I can warrant you good in your glasses, wot about drinking the 'ealth of the bride?'

H. G. Wells *The History of Mr Polly*

Funeral

A funeral was interesting.
It was a real event because there was a ham tea.
And the fact that you got a new coat out of the club money that had been paid.
And there was the drink,
I can remember seeing them put down gold sovereigns.
It was far better than any wedding, was a funeral.
As kids we loved it, the new coat and everything.

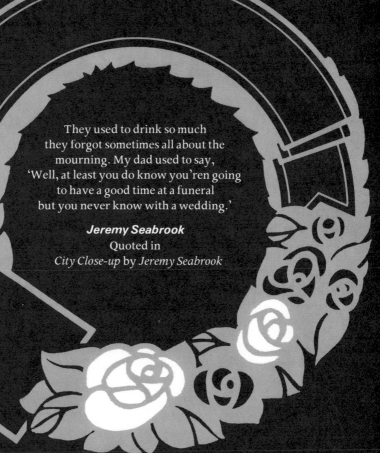

They used to drink so much
they forgot sometimes all about the
mourning. My dad used to say,
'Well, at least you do know you'ren going
to have a good time at a funeral
but you never know with a wedding.'

Jeremy Seabrook
Quoted in
City Close-up by *Jeremy Seabrook*

The Great Tablecloth

When they were called to the table,
the tyrants came rushing
with their temporary ladies;
it was fine to watch the women pass
like wasps with big bosoms
followed by those pale
and unfortunate public tigers.

The peasant in the field ate
his poor quota of bread;
he was alone, it was late,
he was surrounded by wheat,
but he had no more bread;
he ate it with grim teeth,
looking at it with hard eyes.

In the blue hour of eating
the infinite hour of the roast,
the poet abandons his lyre,
takes up his knife and fork,
puts his glass on the table,
and the fishermen attend
the little sea of the soup bowl.
Burning potatoes protest
among the tongues of oil.
The lamb is gold on its coals
and the onion undresses.

It is sad to eat in dinner clothes,
like eating in a coffin,
but eating in convents
is like eating underground.
Eating alone is a disappointment,
but not eating matters more,
is hollow and green, has thorns
like a chain of fish hooks
trailing from the heart,
clawing at your insides.

Hunger feels like pincers,
like the bite of crabs,
it burns, burns and has no fire.
Hunger is a cold fire.
Let us sit down soon to eat
with all those who haven't eaten;
let us spread great tablecloths,
put salt in the lakes of the world,
set up planetary bakeries,
tables with strawberries in snow,
and a plate like the moon itself
from which we can all eat.

For now I ask no more
than the justice of eating.

Pablo Neruda
Translated from the Spanish by Alastair Reid

The Perfect Meal

Daily Telegraph Gallup Poll

1947	1962
Sherry	Sherry
Tomato soup	Tomato soup
Sole	Sole
Roast chicken	Roast chicken
Roast potatoes, peas and sprouts	Roast potatoes, peas and sprouts
Trifle and cream	Fruit salad and cream
Wine	Wine
Coffee	Coffee
Cheese and biscuits	Cheese and biscuits

J. Burnett
Plenty and Want

Mrs Beeton's Picnic

In Mrs Beeton's first edition of 1861
a bill of fare for a picnic for forty persons includes:
A joint of cold roast beef, a joint of cold boiled beef,
2 ribs of lamb, 2 shoulders of lamb, 4 roast fowls, 2 roast ducks,
1 ham, 6 medium-sized lobsters, 1 piece of collared calf's head,
18 lettuces, 6 baskets of salad, 6 cucumbers,
stewed fruit well sweetened and put into glass bottles well corked,
3 or 4 dozen plain pastry biscuits to eat with the stewed fruit,
2 dozen fruit turnovers, 4 dozen cheese cakes,
2 cold cabinet puddings in moulds, a few jam puffs,
1 large cold Christmas pudding (this must be good),
a few baskets of fresh fruit, 3 dozen plain biscuits, a piece of cheese,
6 pounds of butter (this, of course, includes the butter for tea),
4 quartern loaves of household bread, 3 dozen rolls,
6 loaves of tin bread (for tea), 2 plain plum cakes, 2 pound cakes,
2 sponge cakes, a tin of mixed biscuits, half a pound of tea.
Coffee is not suitable for a picnic, being difficult to make.

The list ends with:
Beverages: 3 dozen quart bottles of ale, packed in hampers,
ginger beer, soda-water, and lemonade, of each 2 dozen bottles,
6 bottles of sherry, 6 bottles of claret, champagne at discretion,
and any other light wine that may be preferred,
and 2 bottles of brandy.

Edward VII Breakfast

When in good health,
Edward VII liked to begin each day with a substantial breakfast
(haddock, poached eggs, bacon, chicken and woodcock)
before setting out for a day's shooting or racing.
When in residence, there would be the usual twelve-course
luncheons and dinners, but Edward liked to get out a good deal
to Ascot and Goodwood and to Covent Garden. On these occasions
hampers prepared in the royal kitchens followed him.
At Covent Garden, for example, the King took supper in the
interval from 8.30 p.m. to 9.30 p.m. served in a room at the back
of the royal box: six footmen went down in the afternoon with
cloths, silver and gold plate, and a dozen hampers of food
followed later. For supper there were nine or ten courses,
all served cold: cold consommé, lobster mayonnaise, cold trout,
duck, lamb cutlets, plovers' eggs, chicken, tongue and ham jelly,
mixed sandwiches, three or four desserts made from
strawberries and fresh fruit, ending with French patisserie.

J. Burnett *Plenty and Want*

My Perfect Meal

A big pot of hot pot with plenty of potatoes plenty of liver and
kidneys lots of sausages cooked in the stew and 2 lb of onions
tomatoes mix all together let simmer then add some currie gravy and
a tin of beans then eat, for afters apple crumble custard apple turn
overs custard 4 cups of tea fruit cake one hole one, and then a
packed of match makers and a shandy.

Charles McMillan

My ideal meal is going over the fish shop for 2 saveloys, 1 lot of chips
with crackling and lots of salt and vinegar, then going into the
kitchen, sitting on the rocking (chair) and eating it out of the paper
while watching the telly. I really enjoy this because it has a funny
sort of atmosphere which I cannot explain. I don't know why I like
this the best when there is all those extravagant meals to eat. My 2nd
favourite is pie and mash. I like it because I like sitting in the pie and
mash shop all warm and watching people go past all cold and with
their hands in their pockets, and I am sitting there eating pie and
mash in a lovely warm shop, but it arn't 'arf cold when you go out.

Jeff Sault

A Piece of Pie

Maybe you hear something of this great eating contest that
comes off in New York one night in the early summer of 1937. Of
course eating contests are by no means anything new, and in fact
they are quite an old-fashioned pastime in some sections of this
country, such as the South and East, but this is the first big public
contest of the kind in years, and it creates no little comment along
Broadway. In fact, there is some mention of it in the blats, and it is
not a frivolous proposition in any respect, and more dough is
wagered on it than any other eating contest in history with Joel
Duffle a 6 to 5 favourite over Miss Violette Shumberger all the way
through.

This Joel Duffle comes to New York several days before the contest
with the character by the name of Conway, and requests a meet with
Miss Violette Shumberger to agree on the final details and who shows
up with Miss Violette Shumberger as her coach and adviser but
Nicely-Nicely Jones. Nicely-Nicely Jones used to be a great eating
champion until he got engaged to Miss Hilda Slocum and she forced
him to go on a diet. He is even thinner and more peaked-looking
than when Horsey and I see him last, but he says he feels great, and
that he is within six pounds of his marriage to Miss Hilda Slocum.

Well, it seems that his presence is really due to Miss Hilda Slocum
herself, because she says that after getting her dearest friend Miss
Violette Shumberger into this jackpot, it is only fair to do all she can
to help her win it, and the only way she can think of is to let Nicely-
Nicely give Violette the benefit of his experience and advice.

Futhermore we afterwards learn that when Nicely-Nicely returns to
the apartment on Morningside Heights after giving Violette a lesson,
Miss Hilda Slocum always smells his breath to see if he indulges in
any food during his absence.

Well, this Joel Duffle is a tall character with stooped shoulders, and
a sad expression, and he does not look as if he can eat his way out
of a tea shoppe, but as soon as he commences to discuss the details of
the contest, anybody can see that he knows what time it is in
situations such as this. In fact, Nicely-Nicely says he can tell at once
from the way Joel Duffle talks that he is a dangerous opponent,
and he says while Miss Violette Shumberger impresses him as an
improving eater, he is only sorry she does not have more seasoning.

This Joel Duffle suggests that the contest consist of twelve courses of
strictly American food, each side to be allowed to pick six dishes,
doing the picking in rotation, and specifying the weight and quantity
of the course selected to any amount the contestant making the pick
desires, and each course is to be divided for eating exactly in half,

and after Miss Violette Shumberger and Nicely-Nicely whisper together a while, they say the terms are quite satisfactory.

Then Horsey tosses a coin for the first pick, and Joel Duffle says heads, and it is heads, and he chooses, as the first course, two quarts of ripe olives, twelve bunches of celery, and four pounds of shelled nuts, all this to be split fifty-fifty between them. Miss Violette Shumberger names twelve dozen cherry-stone clams as the second course, and Joel Duffle says two gallons of Philadelphia pepper-pot soup as the third.

Well, Miss Violette Shumberger and Nicely-Nicely whisper together again, and Violette puts in two five-pound striped bass, the heads and tails not to count in the eating, and Joel Duffle names a twenty-two pound roast turkey. Each vegetable is rated as one course, and Miss Violette Shumberger asks for twelve pounds of mashed potatoes with brown gravy. Joel Duffle says two dozen ears of corn on the cob, and Violette replies with two quarts of lima beans. Joel Duffle calls for twelve bunches of asparagus cooked in butter, and Violette mentions ten pounds of stewed new peas.

This gets them down to the salad, and it is Joel Duffle's play, so he says six pounds of mixed green salad with vinegar and oil dressing, and now Miss Violette Shumberger has the final selection, which is the dessert. She says it is a pumpkin pie, two feet across, and not less than three inches deep.

It is agreed that they must eat with knife, fork or spoon, but speed is not to count, and there is to be no time limit, except they cannot pause more than two consecutive minutes at any stage, except in case of hiccoughs. They can drink anything, and as much as they please, but liquids are not to count in the scoring. The decision is to be strictly on the amount of food consumed, and the judges are to take account of anything left on the plates after a course, but not of loose chewings on bosom or vest up to an ounce. The losing side is to pay for the food, and in case of a tie they are to eat it off immediately on ham and eggs only.

Well, the scene of this contest is the second-floor dining room of Mindy's restaurant, which is closed to the general public for the occasion, and only parties immediately concerned in the contest are admitted. The contestants are seated on either side of a big table in the centre of the room, and each contestant has three waiters.

No talking and no rooting from the spectators is permitted, but of course in any eating contest the principals may speak to each other if they wish, though smart eaters never wish to do this, as talking only wastes energy, and about all they ever say to each other is please pass the mustard.

About fifty characters from Boston are present to witness the contest, and the same number of citizens of New York are admitted, and among them is this editor, Mr McBurgle, and he is around asking Horsey if he thinks Miss Violette Shumberger is as good a thing as the jumper at the race track.

Nicely-Nicely arrives on the scene quite early, and his appearance is really most distressing to his old friends and admirers, as by this time he is shy so much weight that he is a pitiful scene, to be sure, but he tells Horsey and me that he thinks Miss Violette Shumberger has a good chance.

'Of course,' he says, 'she is green. She does not know how to pace herself in competition. But,' he says, 'she has a wonderful style. I love to watch her eat. She likes the same things I do in the days when I am eating. She is a wonderful character, too. Do you ever notice her smile?' Nicely-Nicely says.

'But,' he says, 'she is the dearest friend of my fiancée, Miss Hilda Slocum, so let us not speak of this. I try to get Hilda to come to see the contest, but she says it is repulsive. Well, anyway,' Nicely-Nicely says, 'I manage to borrow a few dibs, and am wagering on Miss Violette Shumberger. By the way,' he says, 'if you happen to think of it, notice her smile.'

Well, Nicely-Nicely takes a chair about ten feet behind Miss Violette Shumberger, which is as close as the judges will allow him, and he is warned by them that no coaching from the corners will be permitted, but of course Nicely-Nicely knows this rule as well as they do, and furthermore by this time his exertions seem to have left him without any more energy.

There are three judges, and they are all from neutral territory. One of these judges is a party from Baltimore, MD, by the name of Packard, who runs a restaurant, and another is a party from Providence, RI, by the name of Croppers, who is a sausage manufacturer. The third judge is an old Judy by the name of Mrs Rhubarb, who comes from Philadelphia, and once kept an actors' boarding-house, and is considered an excellent judge of eaters.

Well, Mindy is the official starter, and at 8.30 p.m. sharp, when there is still much betting among the spectators, he outs with his watch, and says like this:

'Are you ready, Boston? Are you ready, New York?'

Miss Violette Shumberger and Joel Duffle both nod their heads, and Mindy says commence, and the contest is on, with Joel Duffle getting the jump at once on the celery and olives and nuts.

It is apparent that this Joel Duffle is one of those rough-and-tumble eaters that you can hear quite a distance off, especially on clams and soups. He is also an eyebrow eater, an eater whose eyebrows go up as high as the part in his hair as he eats, and this type of eater is undoubtedly very efficient.

In fact, the way Joel Duffle goes through the groceries down to the turkey causes the Broadway spectators some uneasiness, and they are whispering to each other that they only wish the old Nicely-Nicely is in there. But personally, I like the way Miss Violette Shumberger eats without undue excitement, and with great zest. She cannot keep close to Joel Duffle in the matter of speed in the early stages of the contest, as she seems to enjoy chewing her food, but I observe that as it goes along she pulls up on him, and I figure this is not because she is stepping up her pace, but because he is slowing down.

When the turkey finally comes on, and is split in two halves right down the middle, Miss Violette Shumberger looks greatly disappointed, and she speaks for the first time as follows:

'Why,' she says, 'where is the stuffing?'

Well, it seems that nobody mentions any stuffing for the turkey to the chef, so he does not make any stuffing, and Miss Violette Shumberger's disappointment is so plain to be seen that the confidence of the Boston characters is somewhat shaken. They can see that a Judy who can pack away as much fodder as Miss Violette Shumberger has to date, and then beef for stuffing, is really quite an eater.

In fact, Joel Duffle looks quite startled when he observes Miss Violette Shumberger's disappointment, and he gazes at her with great respect as she disposes of her share of the turkey, and the mashed potatoes, and one thing and another in such a manner that she moves up on the pumpkin pie on dead-even terms with him. In fact, there is little to choose between them at this point, although the judge from Baltimore is calling the attention of the other judges to a turkey leg that he claims Miss Violette Shumberger does not clean as neatly as Joel Duffle does his, but the other judges dismiss this as a technicality.

Then the waiters bring on the pumpkin pie, and it is without doubt quite a large pie, and in fact it is about the size of a manhole cover, and I can see that Joel Duffle is observing this pie with a strange expression on his face, although to tell the truth I do not care for the expression on Miss Violette Shumberger's face, either.

Well, the pie is cut in two dead centre, and one half is placed before Miss Violette Shumberger and the other half before Joel Duffle, and he does not take more than two bites before I see him loosen his waistband and take a big swig of water, and thinks I to myself, he is now down to a slow walk, and the pie will decide the whole heat, and I am only wishing I am able to wager a little more dough on Miss Violette Shumberger. But about this moment, and before she as much as touches her pie, all of a sudden Violette turns her head and motions to Nicely-Nicely to approach her, and as he approaches, she whispers in his ear.

Now at this, the Boston character by the name of Conway jumps up and claims a foul and several other Boston characters join him in this claim, and so does Joel Duffle, although afterwards even the Boston characters admit that Joel Duffle is no gentleman to make such a claim against a lady.

Well, there is some confusion over this, and the judges hold a conference, and they rule that there is certainly no foul in the actual eating that they can see, because Miss Violette Shumberger does not touch her pie so far.

But they say that whether it is a foul otherwise all depends on whether Miss Violette Shumberger is requesting advice on the contest from Nicely-Nicely and the judge from Providence, R I, wishes to know if Nicely-Nicely will kindly relate what passes between him and Violette so they may make a decision.

'Why,' Nicely-Nicely says, 'all she asks me is can I get her another piece of pie when she finishes the one in front of her.'

Now at this, Joel Duffle throws down his knife, and pushes back his plate with all but two bites of his pie left on it, and says to the Boston characters like this:

'Gentlemen,' he says, 'I am licked. I cannot eat another mouthful. You must admit I put up a game battle, but,' he says, 'it is useless for me to go on against this Judy who is asking for more pie before she even starts on what is before her. I am almost dying as it is, and I do not wish to destroy myself in a hopeless effort. Gentlemen,' he says, 'she is not human.'

Well, of course this amounts to throwing in the old napkin and Nicely-Nicely stands up on his chair, and says:

'Three cheers for Miss Violette Shumberger!'

Then Nicely-Nicely gives the first cheer in person, but the effort overtaxes his strength, and he falls off the chair in a faint just as Joel Duffle collapses under the table, and the doctors at the Clinic Hospital are greatly baffled to receive, from the same address at the same time, one patient who is suffering from undernourishment, and another patient who is unconscious from over-eating.

Well, in the meantime, after the excitement subsides, and wagers are

settled, we take Miss Violette Shumberger to the main floor in Mindy's for a midnight snack, and when she speaks of her wonderful triumph, she is disposed to give much credit to Nicely-Nicely Jones.

'You see,' Violette says, 'what I really whisper to him is that I am a goner. I whisper to him that I cannot possibly take one bite of the pie if my life depends on it, and if he has any bets down to try and hedge them off as quickly as possible.

'I fear,' she says, 'that Nicely-Nicely will be greatly disappointed in my showing, but I have a confession to make to him when he gets out of the hospital. I forget about the contest,' Violette says, 'and eat my regular dinner of pig's knuckles and sauerkraut an hour before the contest starts and,' she says, 'I have no doubt this tends to affect my form somewhat. So,' she says, 'I owe everything to Nicely-Nicely's quick thinking.'

Damon Runyon *Runyon on Broadway*

Demolition Derby

The inspiration for the demolition derby came to Lawrence Mendelsohn one night in 1958 when he was nothing but a square-ribbed twenty-eight-year-old stock-car driver halfway through his tenth lap around the Islip, L.I, Speedway and taking a curve too wide. A lubberly young man with a Chicago boxcar haircut came up on the inside in a 1949 Ford and caromed him twelve rows up into the grandstand, but Lawrence Mendelsohn and his entire car did not hit one spectator.

'That was what got me,' he said, 'I remember I was hanging upside down from my seat belt like a side of Jersey bacon and wondering why no one was sitting where I hit. Lousy promotion,' I said to myself.

'Not only that, but everybody who *was* in the stands forgot about the race and came running over to look at me gift-wrapped upside down in a fresh pile of junk.'...

So why put up with the monotony between crashes?

Such, in brief, is the early history of what is culturally the most important sport ever originated in the United States, a sport that ranks with the gladiatorial games of Rome as a piece of national symbolism. Lawrence Mendelsohn had a vision of an automobile sport that would be all crashes. Not two cars, not three cars, not four cars, but a hundred cars would be out in an arena doing nothing but smashing each other into shrapnel. The car that outrammed and outdodged all the rest, the last car that could still move amid the smoking heap, would take the prize money.

So at 8.15 at night at the Riverhead Raceway, just west of Riverhead, L1, on Route 25, amid the quaint tranquility of the duck and turkey farm flatlands of eastern Long Island, Lawrence Mendelsohn stood up on the back of a flat truck in his red neon warmup jacket and lectured his hundred drivers on the rules and niceties of the new game, the 'demolition derby'. And so at 8.30 the first twenty-five cars moved out onto the raceway's quarter-mile stock-car track. There was not enough room for a hundred cars to mangle each other. Lawrence Mendelsohn's dream would require four heats. Now the twenty-five cars were placed at intervals all about the circumference of the track, making flatulent revving noises, all headed not around the track but toward a point in the center of the infield.

Then the entire crowd, about 4000, started chanting a countdown. 'Ten, nine, eight, seven, six, five, four, three, two,' but it was impossible to hear the rest, because right after 'two' half the crowd went into a strange whinnying wail. The starter's flag went up, and the twenty-five cars took off, roaring into second gear with no mufflers, all headed toward that same point in the centre of the infield, converging nose on nose.

The effect was exactly what one expects that many simultaneous crashes to produce: the unmistakable tympany of automobiles colliding and cheap-gauge sheet metal buckling; front ends folding together at the same cock-eyed angles police photographs of night-time wreck scenes capture so well on grainy paper; smoke pouring from under the hoods and hanging over the infield like a howitzer cloud; a few of the surviving cars lurching eccentrically on bent axles. At last, after four heats, there were only two cars moving through the junk, a 1953 Chrysler and a 1958 Cadillac. In the Chrysler a small fascia of muscles named Spider Ligon, who smoked a cigar while he drove, had the Cadillac cornered up against a guard rail in front of the main grandstand. He dispatched it by swinging around and backing full throttle through the left side of its grille and radiator.

By now the crowd was quite beside itself. Spectators broke through a gate in the retaining screen. Some rushed to Spider Ligon's car, hoisted him to their shoulders and marched off the field, howling. Others clambered over the stricken cars of the defeated, enjoying the details of their ruin, and howling. The good, full cry of triumph and annihilation rose from Riverhead Raceway, and the demolition derby was over.

That was the 154th demolition derby in two years. Since Lawrence Mendelsohn staged the first one at Islip Speedway in 1961, they have been held throughout the United States at the rate of one every five days, resulting in the destruction of about 15,000 cars.

Tommy Fox, who is nineteen, said he entered the demolition derby because, 'You know, it's fun. I like it. You know what I mean?' What was fun about it? 'Well,' he said, 'you know, like when you hit 'em, and all that. It's fun.'

Tom Wolfe *Clean Fun at Riverhead*

Saturday Afternoon

It all started when two of our boyfriends asked us to go to a football match. We said that we might be able to go.

'When is it?'

'On Saturday,' John said. 'Can you go?'

'What football team is it?'

'Millwall.'

'Yes, I should think that I can go.'

'How about you, Chris?'

'Yes, sure I can go.'

'So we will meet here by the lamp-post at 3.15 Saturday afternoon.'

'Yes, we will see you Saturday.' So me and Chris went home. We did not want to be late because of going to the match on Saturday. So I was trying to get round my dad for money. In the end he gave me 5s. And my mum gave me money. So I went up to Chris and then the both of us went to meet the boys. When we got there, the boys were waiting for us. So we just got on a bus and went off. John was wearing Millwall colours, but Dave did not wear anything for Millwall. When we got in the ground we got near the front. There was lots of people there, and we could just about breathe. There was some boys with knives and bottles. Some even had iron bars. But the game was very good. There were only three fights. One boy got a bottle over his head, and was rushed straight to hospital. Three of the boys were taken away by the police. But the game went on very well. There were boys singing 'Cold Blow Lane'. Outside there were all boys waiting to have a big fight, but no one got hurt.

We left Millwall about 6.15, and none of us got home till 8.15. My dad said, 'Who won?' 'We did, 5–0. Don't we always win?'

'Who did they play? Sunderland? Was there a lot of fights?'

'Yes, you should have seen the boys having a go. You should have seen the blood on the floor.'

'Did you enjoy yourself?'

'Yes, it was great! We might go next week. No, not next week, because they are playing away.'

'Never mind, you can go the week after.'

'Great. I will have to tell them, because they won't know. If Chris can't go can I go with John and Dave and my mate Susan?'

'Yes. Sure you can. I will buy you a badge.'

'Roll on next week.'

Susan Varney

Football Match

Then they were in the tunnel running out to the pitch. The crowd directly opposite saw them first, and started the roar which spread round the ground like a forest fire.

Chris crossed the red ash and threw the ball down. The line broke up and the players spurted off at tangents. Lennie sprinted and jogged, sprinted and jogged into the penalty area. Les Adams rolled him a ball. He swung first time and kicked it high over the bar into the kop. Les Adams watched it and the crowd went Woooo! He belted the next one into the top corner. The other team ran out followed by the three officials. The referee carried a shiny orange ball like a Belisha beacon. He placed it on the centre spot and whistled for the captains. Chris lost the toss and the teams changed ends. Lennie looked round the ground and up into the stands. It was a big crowd with no empty spaces at the terrace ends.

The Town inside forwards stood brooding over the ball like three witches. The referee looked at his watch, looked at his officials and blew his whistle. Bobby Prince rolled the ball to Lennie and ran off down the centre. Lennie waited for the rush of the opposing inside men, then back-heeled the ball and slipped between them like stepping through a swinging door. The ball was kicked down the field and the centre half jumped and headed it clear. The crowd roared and settled.

Play was too fast, and both teams tackled too swiftly and often for any pattern or rhythm to be established. Lennie clapped his hands and Chris pushed the ball. He was flat on his face when it reached him. The referee whistled and the opposing right half appealed against the decision with his arms out like an angler. The referee shooed him away and Chris placed the ball for the free kick.

'Push it short, Chris.'

'Get up t'field, Len.'

'Go on, push it short.'

Chris tapped the ball forward, and Lennie dribbled it straight at the right half who had only retreated the necessary ten yards. He kicked it too far in front and the crowd groaned as the right half gained possession. Lennie spurted into the tackle. His foot went over the ball and his fist swung on the blind side of the referee. The right half toppled backwards, holding his stomach as though he had been shot. Lennie retrieved the ball, swerved past a defender and cracked a long, high pass diagonally across the field into the corner. Geordie ran after it, and the full back was back-pedalling so fast that he overbalanced flat on his arse. The crowd screamed. Geordie caught the ball near the corner flag, steadied himself and centred.

The ball swooped down into the penalty area as Lennie ran in to meet it. He flicked his head down to the left and the ball bounced over the goal line near the post.

'G–O–A–L.'

The roar exploded and mushroomed from the ground. Lennie spun round and raised his right arm. Geordie ran in and jumped on his back, and he was smothered under a welter of congratulations. They ran back to their positions as the goalkeeper booted the ball back to the centre, and Lennie trotted past the injured right half who was on the ground receiving treatment from two trainers in tracksuits. He stopped and looked in. 'All right?'

'Piss off! You dirty, fouling bastard.'

Barry Hines *The Blinder*

'Time to go home, everybody – the match ended on Saturday'

Why You Can't Have a
Closet Winger in Sevenoaks

In my childhood your standing in the community depended on how much gear you had. A complete strip plus your own football meant you were cock of the roost with the kind of power unheard of even in modern football management. With it you picked sides, chose which way you wanted to kick, were undisputed ombudsman in all arguments on and off the field, and when things got too hairy you simply terminated proceedings by taking your ball home.

Football boots were bought four sizes too big so that during the first two years of wear you packed the toes with paper waiting for the day when your feet grew into them. But they were treasured. They were not the glove-soft slippers of today but real boots in bullet-proof leather with bulbous shining toes stuck on the end like warheads on guided missiles. They were dubbined and massaged until the leather became semi-soft, but we never touched the toes, which remained hard and lethal until the day they were thrown away or passed on to a younger brother.

The pitches were, in the main, improvised affairs in any quiet street or on any piece of waste ground. The goal-posts were coats and the lack of a crossbar made the award of a goal from a high shot a difficult affair and led to a situation in the Barnsley and District Backyard League where unscrupulous teams would put a midget between the coats and dispute any shot that went above his head. Goal-posts were for adults. Our local side used to dig theirs up after every game and carry them like bullion to a shed where they would be locked away until the next game. They were wooden ones and grew very ancient and were finally replaced after one game when a shot by the opposing centre-forward shattered the crossbar into matchwood and brought the whole structure crashing down on the goalkeeper who was never the same man afterwards.

The new posts were great iron tubes constructed all of a piece. Once planted they were impossible to shift. The club had no option but to leave them standing and we had a marvellous time smacking the crossbar and making it sing like a musical saw. As pitches go it was terrible, but it was the only one we had. It sloped dramatically from one goal line to the other so that the keeper at the top end stood well above the crossbar of his opposite number.

Playing uphill was a nightmare. Winning the ball in the bottom half of the field and moving towards the top end was like scaling the Matterhorn wearing diving boots. Many a breakaway up the hill ended in anti-climax as the brave runner collapsed exhausted on the penalty spot.

The cricket pitch was even more awful, a piece of pasture used by a

local farmer for grazing his cows so that every foray into the outfield was an adventure likely to end in the kind of disaster which has one returning home smelling like a farmyard. The pitch itself would have made a good motor-cycle scramble course. It bred fast bowlers and ruined every batsman who ever played on it. But it didn't matter too much because by the time we graduated to it we had served our apprenticeship on some pretty funny tracks.

My favourite was a narrow strip of land between two houses owned by the man at the chip shop. Its one disadvantage was that anyone playing to leg was in danger of putting the ball into a garden owned by Mrs Clegg, which meant you never got it back and had to abandon the game until someone bought a new ball or pinched one from somewhere. Anyone hitting the ball into her garden was automatically out and this meant that the conditions produced a generation of cricketers who played like angels through the covers but were useless at anything pitched outside leg stump.

We made Mrs Clegg pay for her meanness by pushing unspeakable things through her letterbox on Mischief Night and when she died they found twenty-seven cricket balls in her bottom drawer. May God forgive her.

Michael Parkinson

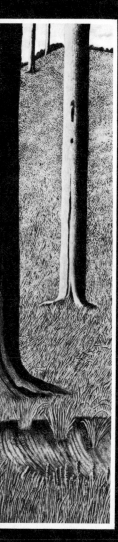

The Tin House

I have a hiding-place over on Laing's building site. It is made of tin. It has a semi-circle shape. It has a funny shaped door which is oblong like but has had the corners chopped off. Inside, it smells of grass and flowers. The roof has a hole on the left-hand side and I sit down on long benches and one of them is broken near the end. The bench is made out of long planks. There is not a tin floor – it is just the ground.

The only place the sun can peep in is the hole and the gaps between the door. All sorts of creatures go in the tin house and weeds are crawling in. The ground is soft and grassy. It is an odd shape and it glinters in the sun. The tin house stands near a wall and some hollyhocks, and the wall is the back of some sheds.

I go there for peace and quiet and sometimes I go there to read books. It is the only place I can go to be on my own. I cannot get much peace now because the builders are building houses and they use drills and cranes. Me and my friends go there as well and we discuss what we are going to do and we also use it for a hiding place when I play outs or hide-and-seek. I go there not too often and not too less. I do not fix up the tin house and it always smells the same and looks the same. It never moves. I suppose the workmen will take it away soon.

It is the greatest place to be. I wish everyone had a tin house. They'd have the time of their life.

Robin Page

117

Let it Flow Joe

Let it flow Joe.

Let your feelings speak for you
Let the people know what you know

Tell the people what it's all about
Shout it out.

When you talk people come alive
People start to realize.

Words flow out of your mouth
When you talk about this earth
Tell the people everything Joe
About what you know.

Talk to them Joe
Let them know
Let the words flow out.

Paul Ritchens

For David Mercer

I like dancers who stamp.
Elegance
Is for certain trees, some birds,
Expensive duchesses, expensive whores,
Elegance, it's a small thing
Useful to minor poets and minor footballers.
But big dancers, they stamp and they stamp fast
Trying to keep their balance on the globe.
Stamp, to make sure the earth's still there,
Stamp, so the earth knows their dancing.

On the music puffs and bangs along beside them
And the dancers sweat, they like sweating
As the lovely drops slide down their scarlet skin
Or shake off into the air
Like notes of music.
I like dancers, like you, who sweat and stamp
And crack the ceiling when they jump.

Adrian Mitchell

Lazybones

They will continue wandering,
these things of steel among the stars,
and weary men will still go up
to brutalize the placid moon.
There, they will found their pharmacies.

In this time of the swollen grape,
the wine begins to come to life
between the sea and the mountain ranges.

In Chile now, cherries are dancing,
the dark mysterious girls are singing,
and in guitars, water is shining.

The sun is touching every door
and making wonder of the wheat.

The first wine is pink in colour,
is sweet with the sweetness of a child,
the second wine is able-bodied,
strong like the voice of a sailor,
the third wine is a topaz, is
a poppy and a fire in one.

My house has both the sea and the earth,
my woman has great eyes
the colour of wild hazelnut,
when night comes down, the sea
puts on a dress of white and green,
and later the moon in the spindrift foam
dreams like a sea-green girl.

I have no wish to change my planet.

Pablo Neruda
Translated from the Spanish by Alastair Reid

Heel and Toe to the End

Gagarin says, in ecstasy
he could have
gone on forever

he floated
ate and sang
and when he emerged from that

one hundred eight minutes off
the surface of
the earth he was smiling

Then he returned
to take his place
from all that division and

subtraction to measure
toe and heel

heel and toe he felt
as if he had
been dancing

William Carlos Williams

Для „Комсомолки"

8365

Acknowledgements

Poems and Prose

For permission to use copyright material acknowledgement is made to the following:

For 'Haiku' and 'When I went Out' by Akahito from *101 Poems from the Japanese* translated by Kenneth Roxroth to Laurence Pollinger Ltd and New Directions; for *Little Big Man* by Thomas Berger to Eyre and Spottiswoode Ltd; for *Adventures of Augie March* by Saul Bellow to Weidenfeld and Nicolson Ltd; for 'A Short History of Oregon' from *Revenge of the Lawn* by Richard Brautigan to Sterling Lord Literary Agency; for 'Saturday Night' by Claude Brown from *Manchild in the Promised Land* to the author; for 'Reckless' and 'Few' from *Let Em Roll Kafka* by Pete Brown to Fulcrum Press; for 'Eeny-Meeny-Miny-Mo' by Andrej Brvar to Modern Poetry in Translation Ltd; for 'I Want to Rediscover the Secret' from *Return to My Native Land* by Aimé Césaire translated by John Berger and Anna Bostock to Presence Africaine; for 'Secondnight in New York City after 3 years' by Gregory Corso from *Selected Poems* to Laurence Pollinger Ltd; for 'The Collector' from *The Whispering Land* by Gerald Durrell to Rupert Hart-Davis; for 'Life with the Marx Brothers' by Allen Eyles from *The Marx Brothers: Their World of Comedy* to the Tantivy Press; for 'Dog' by Lawrence Ferlinghetti from *An Eye on the World* to Macgibbon & Kee Ltd and New Directions; for 'On the Dole' and 'Driving the Bus' from *Work* edited by Ronald Fraser to *New Left Review*; for 'Graffiti' by R.Freeman from *The Marx Brothers: Their World of Comedy* to the Tantivy Press; for 'Tonight at Noon' by Adrian Henri from *The Mersey Sound – Penguin Modern Poets 10* to Deborah Rogers Ltd; for 'Flying a Spitfire' from *The Last Enemy* by Richard Hillary to Macmillan, London and Basingstoke; for 'Excuses' and 'The Football Match' from *The Blinder* by Barry Hines to Michael Joseph Ltd; for 'Poem Title: Two' from *Modern Poetry in Translation 9* by Tamas St Joby to John Batki; for 'Dream of a Black Mother' by Kalungano translated by Philippa Rumsey from *African Writing To-day* edited by Ezekiel Mphahlele © Ezekiel Mphahlele 1967, poem © Kalungano 1967, translation © Philippa Rumsey 1967; for 'Moving Swiftly' by T. E. Lawrence from *Letters to his Biographers* to Cassell & Co. Ltd; for 'Dan Leno' from *Dan Leno Hys Book* to H.Evelyn Ltd; for 'Your Poem, Man . . .' by Edward Lueders from *Some Haystacks Don't Have Any Needle* compiled by Dunning, Lueders and Smith to Scott, Foresman & Co.; for 'At Lunchtime: A Story of Love' by Roger McGough from *Penguin Modern Poets 10* to Hope, Leresche & Steele; for 'Night Fishing' by Andrew Mills to the author; for 'Morning Sunshine' from *The Prison Diary of Ho Chi Minh* translated by Aileen Palmer to Bantam Books; for 'Leaflets' and 'For David Mercer' from *Out Loud* by Adrian Mitchell to Cape Goliard Press; for 'Ode to the Tomato' by Pablo Neruda from *Selected Poems* translated and edited by Nathaniel Tarn to Jonathan Cape and the Estate of the author; for 'Lazybones' by Pablo Neruda from *We are Many* translated by Alastair Reid to Cape Goliard Press and the Estate of the author; for 'The Great Tablecloth' by Pablo Neruda from *Extravaganza* translated by Alastair Reid to Jonathan Cape and the Estate of the author; for 'The Hard Life' by Flann O'Brien to Macgibbon & Kee Ltd; for 'The Tin House' by Robin Page to the author; for 'Why you can't have a closet winger in Sevenoaks' by Michael Parkinson to *Sunday Times*; for 'An Easy Decision' by Kenneth Patchen from *The Collected Poems* to New Directions; for 'The Street Cleaner with his Eighteenth-Century Muck Cart' and 'The Daylight' from *High on the Walls* by Tom Pickard to Fulcrum